Baking Low Carb Bread & Breakfast

By

Diana Lee

Barrington, Illinois 60010

Printed in the U.S.A. by
Cookbooks by Morris Press
P.O. Box 2110 • Kearney, NE 68848

Thank You

I wish to thank my guest authors for allowing me to use their great recipes. They have all contributed greatly to keeping all of us low carbers inspired to lead this healthy life style. Thank you, Dana Carpenter, Barbara Pollack and Jeffrey David.

A special thanks to all you low carbers and low carb list moderators who kept me informed and inspired me to write this cookbook. I can't tell you how much your encouragement kept me going.

Last, but not least, my family. They have all been great testers and even the non carbers contributed by tasting. (I figure if I come up with good enough recipes, they will come over to this healthy lifestyle!) My husband Michael who encouraged me from the beginning to write the first book and put up with my preoccupation and a messy kitchen! My children, Wende, Rick, Kristy and Steve for eating my successes and failures! Thank you.

Before You Begin

Baking low carb is somewhat different than regular baking. You will find that things bake faster and must be watched carefully so they don't become burned or dried out from over baking. Baking with dark bakeware absorbs more heat and may cause foods to cook faster. Dark pans can make breads burn on the outside before the inside is done.

Storing low carb baked goods is also a new ball game. For the most part you will want to keep them in the refrigerator or freezer to prolong their shelf life. If you choose to warm them a little before eating, you may zap them in the microwave but be sure it is for a very short time as again you may dry the food out.

Specific ingredients are called for in my recipes... any substitutes can change the flavor and texture of your recipe.

The ingredients you will be using to bake low carb can be difficult to find if you don't have a health food store, a GNC store or a grocery store that deals in health food products. I will give you some phone numbers and Internet sites that carry these products. When purchasing any ingredients to use while cooking or baking low carb be sure to read labels and choose the one with the lowest carb count.

Recipe Counts - I used Diet Watch to figure the counts on the recipes. They can't be totally accurate as whey protein powders do vary on carb, protein and fiber counts. However, even with these variances you find the counts are close enough for your purposes. To figure an individual serving lets say the total count on a coffee cake is 50 carbs, 4 fiber and 111 protein. You cut the cake into 8 servings. Subtract the fiber from the carbs (46) and divide by servings (8) = approximately 6 carbs per serving. Divide the protein (111) by servings (8) = approximately 14 protein per serving.

Ingredients to have on hand, before you begin, are as follows:

Oat flour can be found in the bread or health food section of your grocery store or at some health food stores. You may also order from CarbSmart at 1-877-279-7091 or at

http://stores.yahoo.com/carbsmart/ or
Walnut Acres at 1-800-433-3998

High Gluten flour or Vital Wheat Gluten is not to be confused with regular gluten flour; it is a wheat flour with starch removed. Read the label and make sure you are getting a gluten flour that is 75% protein and only 6 grams of carbohydrates per 1/4 cup. This can be found in the health food section or bread flour section of your grocery store or at some health food stores. You can also order from CarbSmart at 1-877-279-7091 or http://stores.yahoo.com/carbsmart/. Now Foods in Bloomingdale, IL also distributes to health food stores and http://www.nowfoods.com/ is their web site where they have a way for you to find out where they distribute in your state.

Nuts. An economical place to order nuts for baking is Nuts for U at 800-688-7482 or http://www.nuts4u.com an Internet site.

Peanut Butter should be the natural unsweetened kind with only 6 carbs per two tablespoons.

Liquid sweetener. I mention Sweet & Low as that one is usually the easiest to find at your local grocery store and I use the liquid because it doesn't have any carbohydrates. Also, you will find that combining two different kinds of sweeteners will give you a better taste.

Heavy whipping cream is just that and can be found in the dairy section. Not to be confused with the whipping cream that is already whipped and has sugar added.

Xantham gum is used to thicken and is a fiber so doesn't count as a carbohydrate. This can be found at some health food stores or can be ordered from CarbSmart at 1-877-279-7091 or http://stores.yahoo.com/carbsmart/. You can also order at Gluten-free Pantry 800-291-8386 or check their internet site at http://www.glutenfree.net/.

Baking cocoa is found in the spice and baking section of your grocery store. Choose the one with the lowest carb count on the package.

Splenda can be purchased in the grocery store. The advantage of this sweetener is that it can be used in baking without losing its

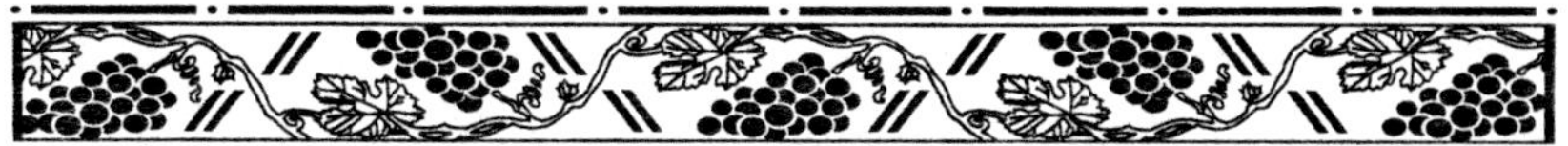

sweetening power and is the best tasting of all the sweeteners. You could probably use a product like Sugar Twin in place of Splenda but you will definitely not get as good a flavor. Can also be ordered at CarbSmart at 1-877-279-7091 or http://stores.yahoo.com/carbsmart/

Vanilla Whey Protein Powder is actually a protein drink. For baking, you want to chose a whey protein powder with a low carbohydrate count 0-4 per serving and with a protein count of 17 or above. It will have a sweetener, xantham gum or guar and flavor. GNC, Walmart, health food stores and some grocery stores carry different brands of whey. Designer Whey Protein and Optimum are a couple of brands and can be found at CarbSmart at 1-877-279-7091 or http://store.yahoo.com/carbsmart.

Natural Whey Protein Powder is a protein drink with no special flavor added. You will want to choose one with a low carbohydrate count 0-4 per serving and with a protein count of 17 or above. It will have no added sweetener, xantham gum or guar, and flavor. GNC, Walmart, health food stores and some grocery stores carry different brands of whey. Designer Whey Protein and Optimum are a couple of brands that can be found at CarbSmart at 1-877-279-7091 or http://store.yahoo.com/carbsmart/

Extracts and spices can be found in your grocery store. However, sometimes it is difficult to find the more exotic extracts so these you can order from Spices, etc. 800-827-6373. Internet site http://www.spicesetc.com. Watkins is another good site and can be reached through http://www.originalvanilla.com/

ThickenThin not/Sugar by Expert Foods. Thickens like cornstarch in shakes, syrups, gravies, sauces and soups -- without the carbs -- and it's much easier to use. Sold at CarbSmart at 1-877-279-7091 or http://store.yahoo.com/carbsmart/ or can be ordered at http://expertfoods.com.

Parchment Paper can be found in your grocery store or kitchen stores. It eliminates the need for pan greasing and helps baked goods to brown evenly on the bottom. Keeps food from sticking.

Questions? I can be emailed through my web site at http://pages.prodigy.net/dls1015/ or you can write me at C.M.I., Diana Lee, 315 W. Northwest Hwy. Palatine, IL 60010

Low Carb Baking Tips

When a recipe calls for beating ingredients together, such as butter, Splenda and eggs, you many need to beat the ingredients a bit longer to get enough air into the mixture to result in a light and even crumb structure.

Low-sugar items bake more quickly than those made with sugar.

Baked goods made with Splenda do not brown like recipes made with sugar. Browning occurs mainly from the reaction of sugar and protein during cooking. Do not wait to see a deep golden brown color on baked goods. Check for doneness using a wooden toothpick. If it comes out clean, it is done.

When replacing Splenda in baked goods, your product will last longer if you store it in the refrigerator. For longer storage, you can freeze baked goods successfully.

For successful leavening (rising) in baked goods, check the expirations dates on your baking powder, baking soda and yeast.

Do not over mix.

Carefully read the recipe before proceeding. Use the specified ingredients and pre-measure them.

Always use metal measuring cups for dry ingredients and a glass measuring cup for liquid ingredients.

Take the time to properly preheat your oven.

Use glass or metal nonstick baking pans, not thin disposable aluminum ones. Baking with dark bakeware absorbs more heat and may cause foods to cook faster. Dark pans can make bread burn on the outside before the inside is done.

For muffin and loaf recipes that require unmolding, place the pan on a wire cake rack and let it stand for 10 minutes. Then unmold.

All bread machines are slightly different. Before starting, read the manufacturers instructions for directions on how to combine ingredients. Some will put the wet ingredients on the top and others will put them on the bottom.

Use parchment paper. This is a must when making low carb crackers and rolls. It eliminates the need for pan greasing. Keeps food from sticking.

Substitutions

I would prefer that you don't substitute because it may make changes to the recipes and the carbohydrate count, but if you want to try, here are some suggestions.
Xanthan Gum- guar gum may be used but reduce the recipe measurement of Xanthan by at least half.

Milk- 1/2 water to 1/2 heavy whipping cream or straight half and half. Carbohydrate counts will be higher with half and half.

Egg- 2 egg yolks + 1 tbl. water = 1 egg. 2 egg whites = 1 egg. 1/4 c. egg substitutes =1 egg.

Butter- margarine, lard, or shortening

Oil- olive oil, vegetable oil, canola oil, or shortening melted.

Baking powder- 1 tsp baking soda + 1/2 tsp. cream of tartar.

Whey Protein Powder- Soy protein powder. Taste will change I would recommend only replacing half with soy. If you use all soy, you many need to increase the water in the recipe.

Oat Flour- Wheat flour will change carbohydrate, protein and fiber counts in recipe and some cases texture. It will add fiber, but has no more nutrients than white flour. Oat has a relatively high protein content and has low gluten. It makes baked goods moister, chewier and more crumbly. Soy Flour is high in protein but has a very strong flavor. May change texture of baked goods. You will probably have to increase the liquid in the recipe and reduce the oven temperature by 25 degrees.

Brown Sugar- 1 tsp. molasses to 1/3 c. brown sugar called for in the recipe.

Sweet & Low- any liquid sweetener with no carbohydrates and that is heat stable.

Sour Cream- 1 tbl. lemon juice, 1 c. cottage cheese, 1/3 c. heavy whipping cream. Blend in a blender or food processor for 2 minutes.

Coffee Drinks

The milk you use will be 1/2 water and 1/2 heavy whipping cream.

Coffee beans should be carefully blended and roasted for espresso. I have used regular decaffeinated coffee beans ground to a fine grind.

Espresso: 1 fluid ounce of straight coffee.

Ammericano: Espresso diluted with hot water until it reaches the volume of 1 cup of coffee.

Spice Ammericano: Add 1/8 tsp. orange peel, 1/8 tsp. lemon peel, dash cinnamon to the coffee grounds before brew ing.

Cappuccino: Espresso topped with one part milk and one part foam.

Mocha: Place sugar free chocolate syrup in bottom of a cup, add espresso, stir, add steamed milk 1/2 inch from top and garnish with whip cream.

Latte: Espresso with steamed milk add to 1-2 inch from the rim of the cup, topped with foam.

Mexican Coffee: Prepare a latte (add a dash of cinnamon to coffee grounds before brewing) and add 1/8 tsp. molasses and 1 tsp Splenda to brewed latte.

Viennese: Add cinnamon to the coffee grounds before brewing the espresso. Prepare a latte with espresso shot, garnish with whipped cream and a dash of cinnamon.

Espresso Macchiato: Espresso topped with a dollop of foam served in a demitasse.

Table of Contents

Yeast Bread & Rolls................1-32

Quick Breads 33-60

Breakfast 61-72

Index

Yeast Bread & Rolls

Breads, Rolls, Kuchen, Sweet Rolls

My Favorite Recipe

YEAST BREAD & ROLLS

BRAN BREAD

(Bread Machine Recommended)

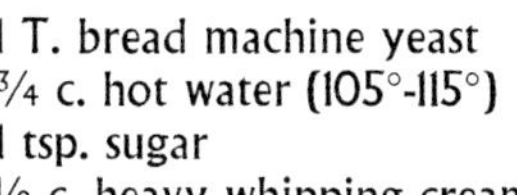

1 T. bread machine yeast
3/4 c. hot water (105°-115°)
1 tsp. sugar
1/2 c. heavy whipping cream
1 T. oil
2 eggs
1/4 c. toasted wheat bran
1 tsp. salt
1 c. Vital wheat gluten flour
1/2 c. oat flour
1 c. natural whey protein powder
1 tsp. xanthan gum

You may use your bread machine with these ingredients. Follow the manufactures directions for the order you add ingredients. Use short bake cycle.

If not using bread machine, sprinkle yeast and sugar in hot water, stir and let it set for a few minutes. Yeast should bubble. If it doesn't then it may be out of date or your water temperature is wrong. In a bowl mix cream, oil, egg and yeast mix together. Add toasted wheat bran, salt, high gluten flour, oat flour, whey protein powder and xanthan gum. Mix well. Dough will be sticky. Cover and put in a warm place until its double in bulk, about 90 to 120 minutes. Prepare a bread pan by spraying with Pam or line with parchment paper. When dough is doubled, put in bread pan and again. Let it rise until double in bulk. Bake at 350° from 35 to 45 minutes.

Note: Total loaf: 85 carbohydrates, 17 fiber, 168 protein.

38656-01

CINNAMON BREAD

(Bread Machine Recommended)

1 T. bread machine yeast
½ c. hot water (105°-115°)
1 tsp. sugar
½ c. heavy whipping cream
1 T. oil
1 egg
¼ c. Splenda
2 tsp. cinnamon
1 tsp. salt
1 c. Vital wheat gluten flour
½ c. oat flour
1 c. vanilla whey protein powder
1 tsp. xanthan gum

You may use your bread machine with these ingredients. Follow the manufacturers directions for the order you add ingredients. Use short bake cycle.

If not using bread machine, sprinkle yeast and sugar in hot water, stir and let it set for a few minutes. Yeast should bubble. If it doesn't then it may be out of date or your water temperature is wrong. In a bowl mix cream, oil, egg and and yeast mix together. Add Splenda, cinnamon, salt, high gluten flour, oat flour, whey protein powder and xanthan gum. Mix well. Dough will be sticky. Cover and put in a warm place until its double in bulk, about 90 to 120 minutes. Prepare a bread pan by spraying with Pam or line with parchment paper. When dough has doubled, put in bread pan and again let it rise until double in bulk. Bake at 350° from 35 to 45 minutes.

Note: Total loaf: 80 carbohydrates, 9 fiber, 187 protein.

38656-01

DILL ONION BREAD
(Bread Machine Recommended)

1 T. bread machine yeast
½ c. hot water (105°-115°)
1 tsp. sugar
½ c. heavy whipping cream
1 T. oil
1 egg
2 tsp. dried dill seed
2 tsp. dried onion flakes
1 tsp. salt
1 c. Vital wheat gluten flour
½ c. oat flour
1 c. natural whey protein powder
1 tsp. xanthan gum

You may use your bread machine with these ingredients. Follow the manufacturer's directions for the order you add ingredients. Use short bake cycle. If not using bread machine, sprinkle yeast and sugar in hot water, stir and let it set for few minutes. Yeast should bubble.

If it doesn't then it may be out of date or your water temperature is wrong. In a bowl mix cream, oil, egg and yeast mix together. Add dried dill seed, dried onion flakes, salt, high gluten flour, oat flour, whey protein powder and xanthan gum. Mix well. Dough will be sticky. Cover and put in a warm place until it is double in bulk, about 90 to 120 minutes. Prepare a greased pan by spraying with Pam or line with parchment paper. When dough has doubled, put in bread pan and again let it raise until double in bulk. Bake at 350° from 35 to 45 minutes.

Note: Total loaf: 77 carbohydrates, 10 fiber, 165 protein.

FLAX BREAD

(Bread Machine Recommended)

1 T. bread machine yeast
¾ c. warm water (105-115°)
1 tsp. sugar
½ c. heavy whipping cream
1 T. oil
1 egg

1 tsp. salt
½ c. ground flax seed
1 c. Vital wheat gluten flour
½ c. oat flour
1 c. natural whey protein powder
1 tsp. xanthan gum

You may use your bread machine with these ingredients. Follow the manufacturer's directions for the order you add ingredients. Use short bake cycle.

If not using bread machine, sprinkle yeast and sugar in hot water, stir and let it set for few minutes. Yeast should bubble. If it doesn't then it may be out of date or your water temperature is wrong. In a bowl mix cream, oil, egg and yeast mix together. Add salt, flax seed, high gluten flour, oat flour whey protein powder and xanthan gum. Mix well. Dough will be sticky. Cover and put in a warm place until it double in bulk, about 90 to 120 minutes. Prepare a bread pan by spraying with Pam or line with parchment paper. When dough has doubled, put in greased pan and again let it raise until double in bulk. Bake at 350° from 35 to 45 minutes.

Note: Total loaf: 84 carbohydrates, 16 fiber, 169 protein.

38656-01

GARLIC BREAD

(Bread Machine Recommended)

1 T. bread machine yeast
½ c. hot water (105°-115°)
1 tsp. sugar
½ c. heavy whipping cream
1 T. oil
1 egg
1 tsp. minced garlic
1 tsp. garlic powder
1 tsp. salt
1 c. Vital wheat gluten flour
½ c. oat flour
1 c. natural whey protein powder
1 tsp. xanthan gum

You may use your bread machine with these ingredients. Follow the manufacturer's directions for the order you add ingredients. Use short bake cycle.

If not using bread machine, sprinkle yeast and sugar in hot water, stir and let it set for a few minutes. Yeast should bubble. If it doesn't, then it may be out of date or your water temperature is wrong. In a bowl mix cream, oil, egg, garlic and yeast mix together. Add garlic powder, salt, high gluten flour, oat flour, whey protein powder and xanthan gum. Mix well. Dough will be sticky. Cover and put in a warm place until its double in bulk, about 90 to 120 minutes. Prepare a bread pan by spraying with Pam or line with parchment paper. When dough has doubled, put in bread pan and again let it rise until double in bulk. Bake at 350° for 35 to 45 minutes.

Note: Total loaf: 77 carbohydrates, 10 fiber and 165 protein.

GINGERBREAD

(Bread Machine Recommended)

1 T. bread machine yeast
½ c. hot water (105°-115°)
1 tsp. sugar
½ c. heavy whipping cream
1 T. oil
1 T. molasses
1 egg
¼ c. Splenda
2 tsp. cinnamon
1 tsp. ginger
¼ tsp. cloves, ground
1 tsp. salt
1 c. Vital wheat gluten flour
½ c. oat flour
1 c. vanilla whey protein powder
1 tsp. xanthan gum

You may use bread machine with these ingredients. Follow the manufacturer's direction for the order you add ingredients. Use short bake cycle.

If not using bread machine, sprinkle yeast and sugar in hot water, stir and let set for few minutes. Yeast should bubble. If it doesn't, then it may be out of date or your water temperature is wrong. In a bowl mix cream, oil, molasses, egg and yeast mix together. Add Splenda, cinnamon, ginger, cloves, salt, high gluten flour, oat flour, whey protein powder and xanthan gum. Mix well. Dough will be sticky. Cover and put in a warm place until its double in bulk, about 90 to 120 minutes. Prepare a bread pan by spraying with Pam or line with parchment paper. When dough has doubled, put in bread pan and again let it raise until double in bulk. Bake at 350° from 35 to 45 minutes.

Note: Total loaf: 89 carbohydrates, 10 fiber and 165 protein.

38656-01

ITALIAN HERB BREAD
(Bread Machine Recommended)

1 T. bread machine yeast
½ c. hot water (105°-115°)
1 tsp. sugar
½ c. heavy whipping cream
1 T. oil
1 egg
1 tsp. dried marjoram
1 tsp. dried basil
1 tsp. dried thyme
1 tsp. salt
1 c. Vital wheat gluten flour
½ c. oat flour
1 c. natural whey protein powder
1 tsp. xanthan gum

You may use your bread machine with these ingredients. Follow the manufacturer's directions for the order you add ingredients. Use short bake cycle.

If not using bread machine, sprinkle yeast and sugar in hot water, stir and let it set for a few minutes. Yeast should bubble. If it doesn't, then it may be out of date or your water temperature is wrong. In a bowl mix cream, oil, egg and yeast mix together. Add marjoram, basil, thyme, salt, high gluten flour, oat flour, whey protein powder and xanthan gum. Mix well. Dough will be sticky. Cover and put in a warm place until its double in bulk, about 90 to 120 minutes. Prepare a bread pan by spraying with Pam or line with parchment paper. When dough has doubled, put in greased pan and again let it raise until double in bulk. Bake at 350° for 35 to 45 minutes.

Note: Total loaf: 77 carbohydrates, 10 fiber, 165 protein.

OAT NUT BREAD

(Bread Machine Recommended)

1 T. bread machine yeast
½ c. hot water (105°-115°)
1 tsp. sugar
½ c. heavy whipping cream
1 T. oil
2 tsp. molasses
1 egg
1 tsp. salt
1 c. Vital wheat gluten flour
½ c. oat flour
1 c. natural whey protein powder
⅓ c. finely chopped walnuts
1 tsp. xanthan gum

You may use your bread machine with these ingredients. Follow the manufactures directions for the order you add ingredients. Use short bake cycle.

If not using bread machine, sprinkle yeast and sugar in hot water, stir and let it set for few minutes. Yeast should bubble. If it doesn't, then it may be out of date or your water temperature is wrong. In a bowl mix cream, oil, molasses, egg and yeast mix together. Add salt, high gluten flour, oat flour, whey protein powder, walnuts and xanthan gum. Mix well. Dough will be sticky. Cover and put in a warm place until it double in bulk, about 90 to 120 minutes. Prepare bread pan by spraying with Pam or line with parchment paper. When dough was doubled, put in bread pan and again let it rise until double in bulk. Bake at 350° from 35 to 45 minutes.

Note: Total loaf: 90 carbohydrates, 14 fiber and 169 protein.

38656-01

ONION AND CHEESE BREAD

(Bread Machine Recommended)

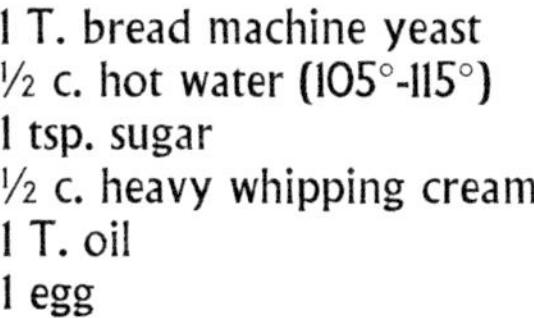

1 T. bread machine yeast
½ c. hot water (105°-115°)
1 tsp. sugar
½ c. heavy whipping cream
1 T. oil
1 egg
2 T. dried onion flakes
⅓ c. grated sharp cheddar cheese
1 tsp. salt
1 c. Vital wheat gluten flour
½ c. oat flour
1 c. natural whey protein powder
1 tsp. xanthan gum

You may use your bread machine with these ingredients. Follow the manufactures directions for the order you add ingredients. Use short bake cycle.

If not using bread machine, sprinkle yeast and sugar into water, stir and let it set for a few minutes. Yeast should bubble. If it doesn't, then it may be out of date or your water temperature is wrong. In a bowl mix cream, oil, egg and yeast mixture together. Add onion flakes, cheese, salt, high gluten flour, oat flour, whey protein powder and xanthan gum. Mix well. Dough will be sticky. Cover and put in a warm place until its double in bulk, about 90 to 120 minutes. Prepare a bread pan by spraying with Pam or line with parchment paper. When dough has doubled, put in bread pan and again let rise until double in bulk. Bake at 350° for 35 to 45 minutes.

Note: Total loaf: 79 carbohydrates, 11 fiber and 177 protein.

PARMESAN GARLIC BREAD

(Bread Machine Recommended)

1 T. bread machine yeast
½ c. hot water (105°-115°)
1 tsp. sugar
½ c. heavy whipping cream
1 T. oil
1 egg
1 tsp. garlic powder
2 tsp. oregano
⅓ c. grated Parmesan cheese
1 tsp. salt
1 c. Vital wheat glutten flour
½ c. oat flour
1 c. natural whey protein powder
1 tsp. xanthan gum

You may use your bread machine with these ingredients. Follow the manufacturer's directions for the order you add ingredients. Use short bake cycle.

If not using bread machine, sprinkle yeast and sugar in hot water, stir and let it set for a few minutes. Yeast should bubble. If it doesn't then it may be out of date or your water temperature is wrong. In a bowl mix cream, oil, egg and yeast mix together. Add garlic powder, oregano, Parmesan cheese, salt, high gluten flour, oat flour, whey protein powder and xanthan gum. Mix well. Dough will be sticky. Cover and put in a warm place until its double in bulk, about 90 to 120 minutes. Prepare a bread pan by spraying with Pam or line with parchment paper. When dough has doubled, put in bread pan and again let it rise until double in bulk. Bake at 350° for 35 to 45 minutes.

Note: Total loaf: 79 carbohydrates, 11 fiber and 177 protein.

38656-01

PUMPERNICKEL

(Bread Machine Recommended)

1 T. bread machine yeast
½ c. hot water (105°-115°)
1 tsp. sugar
½ c. heavy whipping cream
1 T. oil
1 egg
1 T. molasses
2 tsp. instant coffee granules
2 T. cocoa
2 T. Splenda
1 tsp. salt
1 c. Vital wheat gluten flour
½ c. rye flour
1 c. natural whey protein powder
1 tsp. xanthan gum

You may use your bread machine with these ingredients. Follow the manufacturer's directions for the order you add ingredients. Set short bake cycle.

If not using bread machine, sprinkle yeast and sugar in hot water, stir and let it rest for a few minutes. Yeast should bubble. If it doesn't, then it may be out of date or your water temperature is wrong. In a bowl mix cream, oil, egg, molasses, instant coffee and yeast mix together. Add cocoa, Splenda salt, high gluten flour, rye flour, whey protein powder and xanthan gum. Mix well. Dough will be sticky. Cover and put in a warm place until its double in bulk, about 90 to 120 minutes. Prepare a bread pan by spraying with Pam or line with parchment paper. When dough has doubled, put in bread pan and again let it rise until double in bulk. Bake at 350° for 35 to 45 minutes.

Note: Total loaf: 113 carbohydrates, 10 fiber and 167 protein.

RANCH BREAD

(Bread Machine Recommended)

1 T. bread machine yeast
½ c. hot water (105°-115°)
1 tsp. sugar
½ c. heavy whipping cream
1 T. oil
1 egg
2 T. Hidden Valley Ranch dressing mix
½ tsp. salt
1 c. Vital wheat gluten flour
½ c. oat flour
1 c. natural whey protein powder
1 tsp. xanthan gum

You may use your bread machine with these ingredients. Follow the manufacturers directions for the order you add ingredients. Use short bake cycle.

If not using bread machine, sprinkle yeast and sugar in hot water, stir and let it set for a few minutes. Yeast should bubble. If it doesn't then it may be out of date or your water temperature is wrong. In a bowl mix cream, oil, eggs and yeast mix together. Add Ranch dressing mix, salt, high gluten flour, oat flour, whey protein powder and xanthan gum. Mix well. Dough will be sticky. Cover and put in a warm place until its double in bulk, about 90 to 120 minutes. Prepare a bread pan by spraying with Pam or line with parchment paper. When dough has doubled, put in bread pan and again let it rise until double in bulk. Bake at 350° for 35 to 45 minutes.

Note: Total loaf: 82 carbohydrates, 10 fiber and 165 protein.

38656-01

RYE BREAD
(Bread Machine Recommended)

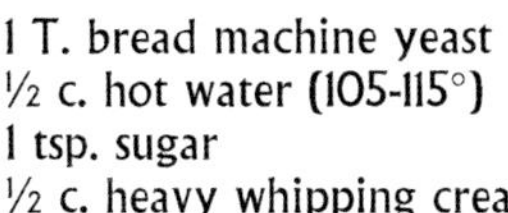

1 T. bread machine yeast
½ c. hot water (105-115°)
1 tsp. sugar
½ c. heavy whipping cream
1 T. oil
1 egg
1 tsp. molasses
1 T. caraway seeds
1 tsp. salt
1 c. Vital wheat gluten flour
½ c. rye flour
1 c. natural whey protein powder
1 tsp. xanthan gum

You may use your bread machine with these ingredients. Follow the manufacturer's directions for the order you add ingredients. Use short bake cycle.

If not using bread machine, sprinkle yeast and sugar in hot water, stir let it set for a few minutes. Yeast should bubble. If it doesn't, then it may be out of date or your water temperature is wrong. In a bowl mix cream, oil, egg, molasses and yeast mix together. Add caraway seeds, salt, high gluten flour, rye flour, whey protein powder and xanthan gum. Mix well. Dough will be sticky. Cover and put in a warm place until its double in bulk, about 90 to 120 minutes. Prepare a bread pan by spraying with Pam or line with parchment paper. When dough has doubled, put in bread pan and again let it rise until double in bulk. Bake at 350° for 35 to 45 minutes.

Note: Total loaf: 95 carbohydrates 17 fiber and 165 protein.

Baking Low Carb Bread & Breakfast

SPICY SWEET BREAD

(Bread Machine Recommended)

1 T. bread machine yeast
½ c. hot water (105°-115°)
1 tsp. sugar
½ c. heavy whipping cream
1 T. oil
1 egg
1 tsp. molasses
¼ c. Splenda
2 tsp. cinnamon
1 tsp. nutmeg
1 tsp. salt
1 c. Vital wheat gluten flour
½ c. oat flour
1 c. vanilla whey protein powder
1 tsp. xanthan gum

You may use your bread machine with these ingredients. Follow the manufacturer's directions for the order you add ingredients. Use short bake cycle.

If not using bread machine, sprinkle yeast and sugar in hot water, stir and let it set for few minutes. Yeast should bubble. If it doesn't, then it may be out of date or your water temperature is wrong. In a bowl mix cream, oil, egg, molasses and yeast mix together. Add Splenda, cinnamon, nutmeg, salt, high gluten flour, oat flour, whey protein powder and xanthan gum. Mix well. Dough will be sticky. Cover and put in a warm place until its double in bulk, about 90 to 120 minutes. Prepare a bread pan by spraying with Pam or line with parchment paper. When dough has doubled, put in bread pan and again let it rise until double in bulk. Bake at 350° for 35 to 45 minutes.

Note: Total loaf: 84 carbohydrates, 12 fiber and 165 protein.

38656-01

TOMATO ROSEMARY BREAD

(Bread Machine Recommended)

1 T. bread machine yeast
½ c. hot water (105°-115°)
1 tsp. sugar
½ c. heavy whipping cream
1 T. oil
1 egg
3 T. snipped unsalted dried tomatoes
1 tsp. rosemary
¾ tsp. paprika
1 tsp. salt
1 c. Vital Wheat gluten flour
½ c. oat flour
1 c. natural whey protein powder
1 tsp. xanthan gum

You may use your bread machine with these ingredients. Follow with manufacturer's directions for the order you add ingredients. Use short bake cycle.

If not using bread machine, sprinkle yeast and sugar in hot water, stir and let it set for a few minutes. Yeast should bubble. If it doesn't, then it may be out of date or your water temperature is wrong. In a bowl mix cream, oil, egg and yeast mix together. Add dried tomatoes, rosemary, paprika, salt, high gluten flour oat flour, whey protein powder and xanthan gum. Mix well. Dough will set sticky. Cover and put in warm place until its double in bulk, about 90 to 120 minutes. Prepare a bread pan by spraying with Pam or line with parchment paper. When dough has doubled, put in bread pan and again let it rise until double in bulk. Bake at 350° for 35 to 45 minutes.

Note: Total loaf: 78 carbohydrates, 10 fiber and 167 protein.

38656-01

WHEAT BREAD

(Bread Machine Recommended)

1 T. bread machine yeast
½ c. hot water (105°-115°)
1 tsp. sugar
½ c. heavy whipping cream
1 T. oil
1 egg
3 T. Sweet 'N Low Spoonable brown sugar
1 tsp. salt
1 c. Vital wheat gluten flour
½ c. whole-wheat flour
1 c. natural whey protein powder
1 tsp. xanthan gum

You may use your bread machine with these ingredients. Follow the manufacturer's directions for the order you add ingredients. Use short bake cycle.

If not using bread machine, sprinkle yeast and sugar in hot water, stir and let it set for a few minutes. Yeast should bubble. If it doesn't then it may be out of date or your water temperature is wrong. In a bowl mix cream, oil, egg and yeast mix together. Add brown sugar, salt, high gluten flour, wheat flour, whey protein powder and xanthan gum. Mix well. Dough will be sticky. Cover and put in a warm place until its double in bulk, about 90 to 120 minutes. Prepare a bread pan by spraying with Pam or line with parchment paper. When dough has doubled, put in bread pan and again let it rise until double in bulk. Bake at 350° for 35 to 45 minutes.

Note: Total loaf: 77 carbohydrates, 9 fiber and 168 protein.

38656-01

WHITE BREAD

(Bread Machine Recommended)

Yeast Bread & Rolls

1 T. bread machine yeast
½ hot water (105°-115°)
1 tsp. sugar
½ c. heavy whipping cream
1 T. oil
1 egg
1 tsp. salt
1 c. Vital wheat gluten flour
½ c. oat flour
1 c. natural whey protein powder
1 tsp. xanthan gum

You may use your bread machine with these ingredients. Follow the manufacturer's directions for the order you add ingredients. Use short bake cycle.

If not using bread machine, sprinkle yeast and sugar in hot water, stir and let it set for a few minutes. Yeast should bubble. If it doesn't, then it may be out of date or your water temperature is wrong. In a bowl mix cream, oil, egg and yeast mix together. Add salt, high gluten flour, oat flour, whey protein powder and and xanthan gum. Mix well. Dough will be sticky. Cover and put in a warm place until its double in bulk, about 90 to 120 minutes. Prepare a bread pan by spraying with Pam or line with parchment paper. When dough has doubled, put in bread pan and again let rise until double in bulk. Bake at 350° from 35 to 45 minutes.

Note: Total loaf: 74 carbohydrates, 10 fiber and 165 protein.

38656-01

SQUARE HAMBURGER BUNS

(Bread Machine Recommended)

1 T. bread machine yeast
½ c. hot water (105°-115°)
1 tsp. sugar
⅓ c. heavy whipping cream
2 T. soft butter
1 egg
2 tsp. butter extract
1 tsp. salt
1 c. Vital wheat gluten flour
½ c. oat flour
½ c. natural whey protein powder
1 tsp. xanthan gum

Use your bread machine with these ingredients. Follow the manufacturer's directions for the order you add ingredients Set the machine for dough cycle.

If not using the bread machine, sprinkle the yeast and sugar in hot water, stir and let it set for a few minutes. Yeast should bubble. If it doesn't, then it may be out of date or your water temperature is wrong. In a bowl, mix cream, butter, eggs, extract, salt and yeast together. Add salt, Vital wheat gluten flour, oat flour, whey protein powder and xanthan gum. Mix at low speed for 3 minutes. Scrape from sides of bowl and form the best ball you can as dough will be sticky. Cover and put in a warm place until it is double in bulk. (I turn the oven to its lowest degree while I prepare the dough and then turn it off and place covered dough in the oven to rise.) Will take 90 to 120 minutes to rise. If you wish to make the rolls at a later time you may place covered dough in refrigerator.

When you remove the dough, you will then let it rise until it is double in bulk. Will take 90 to 120 minutes to rise. When dough has doubled, remove the dough and roll out between two pieces of parchment paper or you can stretch and pat it. Make a rectangle. Dough should be between ½ inch and ¾ inch thick, cut into 10 squares you should end up with 10 rolls. Place on Pam or greased cookie sheet, cover and let rise until doubled in bulk. Will take 90 to 120 minutes. Bake at 350° for 8 to 10 minutes. Brush with melted butter.

Note: Total recipe: 66 carbohydrates, 8 fiber and 146 protein.

38656-01

DINNER ROLLS

(Bread Machine Recommended)

1 T. bread machine yeast
½ c. hot water (105°-115°)
1 tsp. sugar
⅓ c. heavy whipping cream
2 T. soft butter
1 egg
2 tsp. butter extract
1 tsp. salt
1 c. Vital wheat gluten flour
½ c. oat flour
½ c. natural whey protein powder
1 tsp. xanthan gum

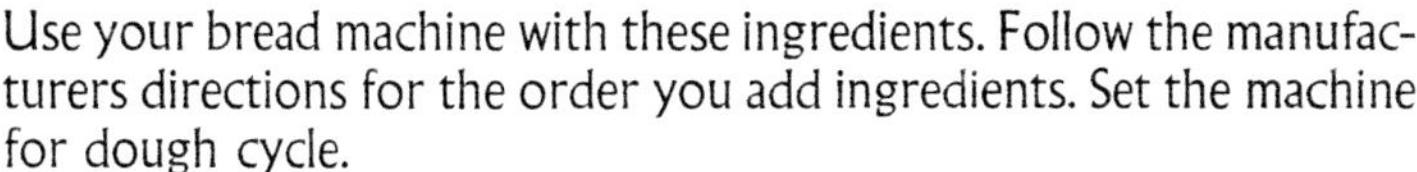

Use your bread machine with these ingredients. Follow the manufacturers directions for the order you add ingredients. Set the machine for dough cycle.

If not using the bread machine, sprinkle the yeast and sugar in hot water, stir and let it set for a few minutes. Yeast should bubble. If it doesn't then it may be out of date or your water temperature is wrong. In a bowl, mix cream, butter, egg, extract, salt and yeast together. Add salt, Vital wheat gluten flour, oat flour, whey protein powder and xanthan gum. Mix at low speed for 3 minutes. Scrape from sides of bowl and form the best ball you can as dough will be sticky. Cover and put in a warm place until it is double in bulk. (I turn the oven to its lowest degree while I prepare the dough and then turn it off and place covered dough in the oven to rise.) Will take 90 to 120 minutes to rise. If you wish to make the rolls at a later time, you may place covered dough in refrigerator.

When you remove the dough, you will then let it rise until it is double in bulk. Will take 90 to 120 minutes to rise. When dough has doubled, remove the dough and roll out between two pieces of parchment paper or you can stretch and pat. Dough should be between ½ to ¾ inch thick, cut into 3-inch circles using a glass or a biscuit cutter. You should end up with 12 rolls. Place on Pam or greased cookie sheet, cover and let rise until double in bulk. Will take 90 to 120 minutes. Bake at 350° for 8 to 10 minutes. Brush with melted butter.

Note: Total recipe: 66 carbohydrates, 8 fiber and 146 protein.

38656-01

RYE DINNER ROLLS

(Bread Machine Recommended)

1 T. bread machine yeast
½ c. hot water, 105°-115°
1 tsp. sugar
⅓ c. heavy whipping cream
2 T. soft butter
1 egg
2 tsp. butter extract
1 tsp. molasses
1 tsp. salt
1 c. Vital wheat gluten flour
½ c. rye flour
½ c. natural whey protein powder
1 tsp. xanthan gum

Use your bread machine with these ingredients. Follow the manufacturer's directions for the order you add ingredients. Set the machine for dough cycle.

If not using the bread machine, sprinkle the yeast and sugar in hot water, stir and let it set for a few minutes. Yeast should bubble. If it doesn't then it may be out of date or you water temperature is wrong. In a bowl, mix cream, butter, egg, extract, molasses, salt and yeast together. Add salt, Vital wheat gluten flour, rye flour, whey protein powder and xanthan gum. Mix at slow speed for 3 minutes. Scrape from sides of bowl and form the best ball you can as dough will be sticky. Cover and put in a warm place until it is double in bulk. (I turn the oven to its lowest degree while I prepare the dough and then turn it off and place covered dough in the oven to rise.) Will take 90 to 120 minutes to rise. If you wish to make the roll at a later time you may place covered dough in refrigerator.

When you remove the dough, you will then let it rise until it is double in bulk. Will take 90 to 120 minutes to rise. When dough has doubled, remove the dough and roll out between two pieces of parchment paper or you can stretch and pat it. Dough would be between ½ and ¾ inch thick, cut into 3-inch circle using a glass or biscuit cutter. You should end up with 12 rolls. Place on Pam or greased cookie sheet, cover and let rise until double in bulk. Will take 90 to 120 minutes. Bake at 350° for 8 to 10 minutes. Brush with melted butter.

Note: Total recipe: 70 carbohydrates, 9 fiber and 146 protein.

38656-01

SOUR CREAM KUCHEN

(Bread Machine Recommended)

Parchment paper
1 T. bread machine yeast
½ c. warm water (105°-115°)
1 tsp. sugar
⅓ c. heavy whipping cream
2 T. soft butter
1 egg
1 tsp. almond extract
3 T. Splenda
1 c. Vital wheat gluten flour
½ c. oat flour
½ c. vanilla whey protein powder
1 tsp. xanthan gum

Use your bread machine with these ingredients. Follow the manufacturer's directions for the order you add ingredients. Set the machine for dough cycle.

If not using the bread machine, sprinkle the yeast and sugar in hot water, stir and let it set for a few minutes. Yeast should bubble. If it doesn't then it may be out of date or your water temperature is wrong. In a bowl, mix cream, butter, egg, almond extract and yeast together. Add Splenda, Vital wheat gluten flour, oat flour, vanilla, whey protein powder, xanthan gum and cinnamon. Mix at low speed for 3 minutes. Scrape from sides of bowl and from the best ball you can as dough will be sticky. Cover and put in a warm place until it is double in bulk. (I turn the oven to its lowest degree while I prepare the dough and then turn it off and place covered dough and then turn it off and place covered dough in the oven to rise.) Will take 90 to 120 minutes to rise.

Place dough in 9-inch round pan and let it rise until double in bulk.

Topping:

⅓ c. sour cream
3 T. Splenda
½ tsp. Sweet 'N Low brown sugar
½ tsp. cinnamon

Using thumb put as many as possible indentations in top of raised dough. Fill indentations with sour cream, smooth over top of dough. Sprinkle the top of the dough with Splenda, Sweet 'N Low brown sugar, ½ teaspoon cinnamon that has been mixed together. Bake at 375° for 25 to 30 minutes.

Note: Total recipe: 72 carbohydrates, 6 fiber and 148 protein.

RHUBARB KUCHEN

(Bread Machine Recommended)

1 T. bread machine yeast
Parchment paper
½ c. warm water (105-115°)
1 tsp. sugar
⅓ c. heavy whipping cream
2 T. soft butter
1 egg
1 tsp. almond extract
3 T. Splenda
1 c. Vita wheat gluten flour
½ c. oat flour
½ c. vanilla whey protein powder
1 tsp. xanthan gum

Use your bread machine with these ingredients. Follow the manufacturer's directions for the order you add ingredients. Set the machine for dough cycle.

If not using the bread machine, sprinkle the yeast and sugar in hot water, stir and let it set for a few minutes. Yeast should bubble. If it doesn't then it may be out of date or your water temperature is wrong. In a bowl, mix cream, butter, egg, almond extract and yeast together. Add Splenda, Vital wheat gluten flour, oat flour, vanilla whey protein powder, xanthan gum and cinnamon. Mix at slow speed for 3 minutes. Scrape from sides of bowl and form the best ball you can dough will be sticky. Cover and put in a warm place until it is double in bulk. (I turn the oven to its lowest degree while I prepare the dough and then turn it off and place covered dough in the oven to rise.) Will take 90 to 120 minutes to rise.

Place dough in 9-inch round pan and let it rise until double in bulk.

Topping:

1 beaten egg yolk
1 T. heavy whipping cream
½ c. Splenda
1 tsp. cinnamon
1½ c. thinly sliced rhubarb

Mix together egg yolk, cream, Splenda and cinnamon. Stir in rhubarb. Using thumb put as many as possible indentations in top of raised dough. Fill indentations with rhubarb mix; smooth over top of dough. Bake at 375° for 25 to 30 minutes.

Note: Total recipe: 86 carbohydrates, 10 fiber and 154 protein.

38656-01

APPLE CIDER ROLLS

(Bread Machine Recommended)

1 T. bread machine yeast
Parchment Paper
½ c. warm water (105°-115°)
1 tsp. sugar
⅓ c. heavy whipping cream
2 T. soft butter
1 egg
2 T. Splenda
1 c. Vital wheat gluten flour
½ c. oat flour
½ c. vanilla whey protein powder
1 tsp. xanthan gum
1 tsp. cinnamon

Use your bread machine with these ingredients. Follow the manufacturer's directions for the order you add ingredients. Set the machine for dough cycle.

If not using the bread machine, sprinkle the yeast and sugar in warm water, stir and let it set for a few minutes. Yeast should bubble. If it doesn't, then it may be out of date or your water temperature is wrong. In a bowl, mix cream butter, egg and yeast together. Add Splenda, Vital wheat gluten flour, oat flour, vanilla whey protein powder, xanthan gum and cinnamon. Mix at slow speed for 3 minutes. Scrape from sides of bowl and form the best ball you can as dough will be sticky. Cover and put in a warm place until it is double in bulk. (I turn the oven to its lowest degree while I prepare the dough and then turn it off and place covered dough in the oven to rise) Will take 90 to 120 minutes to rise. If you wish to make the rolls at a later time you may place covered in refrigerator. When you remove the dough, you will then let it rise until its double in bulk. Will take 90 to 12 minutes to rise.

When dough has doubled, remove the dough and roll out between two pieces of parchment paper in a rectangle shape, approximately 12 x 10 inches.

Filling:

½ c. butter
1 pkg. Alpine sugar free spiced cider
1 T. Sugar Twin Spoonable brown sugar

Melt butter and pour ¼ cup into a 9 x 13-inch pan. Spread the rest on rolled out dough. Combine 1 package Alpine sugar free spiced cider and 1 tablespoon Sugar Twin Spoonable brown sugar. Sprinkle over buttered dough. Roll rectangle up tightly, beginning at 12-inch side. Pinch edge of dough into roll to seal. Stretch and shape until even. Cut roll into 12 pieces. Place slightly apart in buttered 9 x 12-inch pan. Brush with melted butter and let rise 90 to 120 minutes until again double in bulk. Bake at 350° oven for 10 to 15 minutes until light brown. Remove from oven and immediately invert pan on a sheet of wax paper. Cool.

Note: Total recipe is 75 carbohydrates, 8 fiber, 146 protein without frosting. Cream cheese frosting is good on these. See index for recipe. Makes 12 servings.

BISMARCKS

(Bread Machine Recommended)

Parchment paper
1 T. bread machine yeast
½ c. warm water (105°-115°)
1 tsp. sugar
⅓ c. heavy whipping cream
2 T. soft butter
1 egg
3 T. Splenda
1 c. Vital wheat gluten flour
½ c. oat flour
½ c. vanilla whey protein powder
1 tsp. xanthan gum

Use your bread machine with these ingredients. Follow the manufacturer's directions for the order you add ingredients. Set the machine for dough cycle.

If not using the bread machine, sprinkle the yeast and sugar in hot water, stir and let it set for a few minutes. Yeast should bubble. If it doesn't, then it may be out of date or your water temperature is wrong. In a bowl, mix cream, butter, egg and yeast together. Add Splenda, Vital wheat gluten flour, oat flour, vanilla, whey protein powder, xanthan gum and cinnamon. Mix at slow speed for 3 minutes. Scrape from sides of bowl and form the best ball you can as dough will be sticky. Cover and put in a warm place until it is double in bulk. (I turn the oven to its lowest degree while I prepare the dough and then turn if off and place covered dough in the oven to rise.) Will take 90 to 120 minutes to rise. If you wish to make the roll at a later time you may place covered dough in refrigerator. When you remove the dough you will then let it rise until it is double in bulk. Will take 90 to 120 minutes to rise.

When dough has doubled, remove the dough and roll out between two pieces of parchment paper or you can stretch and pat it. Dough should be between ½ inch and ¾ inch thick. Cut into 3-inch circles using a glass or a biscuit cutter. You should end up with 12 rolls. Place on Pam or greased cookie sheet, cover and let rise until double in bulk. Will take 90 to 120 minutes. After rolls have risen, fry in deep hot fat (375°), turning once until light brown. Only fry a few at a time. Drain on paper towel and cool. Cut a slit in the side of each roll and use a cake decorating tube with a narrow point or a spoon to insert your favorite low carbohydrate jam, whipped cream or pudding. Drizzle with a Glaze. See Index for recipes.

Note: Total recipe without filling is 69 carbohydrates, 8 fiber and 146 protein. Makes 12 servings.

38656-01

CHOCOLATE FILLED DANISH ROLLS

(Bread Machine Recommended)

Parchment paper
1 T. bread machine yeast
½ c. warm water (105°-115°)
1 tsp. sugar
⅓ c. heavy whipping cream
2 T. soft butter
1 egg
1 tsp. almond extract
3 T. Splenda
1 c. Vital wheat gluten flour
½ c. oat flour
½ c. vanilla whey protein powder
1 tsp. xanthan gum

Use your bread machine with these ingredients. Follow the manufacturer's directions for the order you add ingredients. Set the machine for dough cycle.

If not using the bread machine, sprinkle the yeast and sugar in hot water, stir and let it set for a few minutes. Yeast should bubble. If it doesn't then it may be out of date or your water temperature is wrong. In a bowl, mix cream butter, eggs, almond extract and yeast together. Add Splenda, Vital wheat gluten flour, oat flour, vanilla whey protein powder, xanthan gum and cinnamon. Mix at slow speed for 3 minutes. Scrape from sides of bowl and from the best ball you can as dough will be sticky. Cover and put in a warm place until it is double in bulk. (I turn the oven to its lowest degree while I prepare the dough and then turn it off and place covered dough in the oven to rise.) Will take 90 to 120 minutes to rise. If you wish to make the rolls at a later time you may place covered dough in refrigerator. When you remove the dough, you will then let it rise until it is double in bulk. Will take 90 to 120 minutes.

When dough has doubled, remove the dough and roll out between two pieces of parchment paper or you can stretch and pat it. Dough should be between ½ inch and ¾ inch thick, cut into 3-inch circle using a glass or a biscuit cutter. You should end up with 12 rolls. Place on Pam or greased cookie sheet, cover and let rise until double in bulk. Will take 90 to 120 minutes.

Filling:

1 regular pkg. sugar free chocolate pie filling NOT INSTANT prepared according to pkg. directions
1 c. water
1 c. heavy whipping cream

After rolls have risen, make indentation about 1 inch wide in center of each ball, pressing to bottom. Fill each with 1 to 2 tablespoons pie filling. Bake 8 to 10 minutes at 350°. Remove from oven and drizzle with a glaze. See index for recipe. You won't use all the pudding so my carbohydrates figures are with 1 cup of the pudding used.

Note: Total recipe is 89 carbohydrates, 10 fiber and 149 protein. Makes 12 servings.

CINNAMON ROLLS

(Bread Machine Recommended)

Baking Low Carb Bread & Breakfast

Parchment paper
1 T. bread machine yeast
½ c. warm water (105°-115°)
1 tsp. sugar
⅓ c. heavy whipping cream
2 T. soft butter
1 egg
2 T. Splenda
1 c. Vital wheat gluten flour
½ c. oat flour
½ c. vanilla whey protein powder
1 tsp. xanthan gum
1 tsp. cinnamon

Use your bread machine with these ingredients. Follow the manufacturer's directions for the order you add ingredients. Set the machine for dough cycle.

If not using the bread machine, sprinkle the yeast and sugar in warm water, stir and let it set for a few minutes. Yeast should bubble. If it doesn't, then it may be out of date or your water temperature is wrong. In a bowl, mix cream, butter, eggs and yeast together. Add Splenda, Vital wheat gluten flour, oat flour, vanilla whey protein powder, xanthan gum and cinnamon. Mix at slow speed for 3 minutes. Scrape from sides of bowl and form the best ball you can as dough will be sticky. Cover and put in a warm place until it is double in bulk. (I turn the oven to its lowest degree while I prepare the dough and then turn it off and place covered dough in the oven to rise.) Will take 90 to 120 minutes to rise. If you wish to make the rolls at a later time you may place covered dough in refrigerator. remove the dough, you will then let it rise until it is double in bulk. Will take 90 to 120 minutes to rise.

When dough has doubled, remove the dough and roll out between two pieces of parchment paper in a rectangle shape, approximately 12 x 10 inches.

Filling;

½ c. butter
¼ c. Splenda
½ tsp. cinnamon
1 tsp. Sugar Twin Spoonable brown sugar

Melt butter and pour ¼ cup into a 9 x 13-inch pan. Spread the rest of rolled out dough. Combine ¼ cup Splenda, ½ teaspoons cinnamon and 1 teaspoon Sugar Twin Spoonable brown sugar. Sprinkle over buttered dough. Roll rectangle up tightly, beginning at 12-inch side. Pinch edge of dough into roll to seal. Stretch and shape until even. Cut roll into 12 pieces. Place slightly apart in buttered 9 x 10-inch pan. Brush with melted butter and let rise 90 to 120 minutes until again double in bulk. Bake at 350° for 10 to 15 minutes until light brown. Remove from oven and immediately invert pan on a sheet of wax paper. Cool.

Note: Total Recipe is 77 carbohydrates, 8 fiber and 146 protein without frosting. Cream Cheese Frosting is good on these. See index for recipe. Makes 12 servings.

38656-01

CREAM CHEESE DANISH ROLLS

(Bread Machine Recommended)

Parchment paper
1 T. bread machine yeast
½ c. warm water (105°-115°)
1 tsp. sugar
⅓ c. heavy whipping cream
2 T. soft butter
1 egg
1 tsp. almond extract
3 T. Splenda
1 c. Vital wheat gluten flour
½ c. oat flour
½ c. vanilla whey protein powder
1 tsp. xanthan gum

Use your bread machine with these ingredients. Follow the manufacturer's directions for the order you add ingredients. Set the machine for dough cycle.

If not using the bread machine, sprinkle the yeast and sugar in hot water, stir and let it set for a few minutes. Yeast should bubble. If it doesn't, then it may be out of date or your water temperature is wrong. In a bowl, mix cream, butter, egg, almond extract and yeast together. Add Splenda, Vital wheat gluten flour, oat flour, vanilla whey protein powder xanthan gum and cinnamon. Mix at low speed for 3 minutes. Scrape from sides of bowl and form the best ball you can as dough will be sticky. Cover and put in a warm place until it is double in bulk. (I turn the oven to its lowest degree while I prepare the dough and then turn it off and place covered dough in the oven to rise.) Will take 90 to 120 minutes to rise. If you wish to make the rolls at a later time you may place covered dough in refrigerator. When you remove the dough you will then let it rise until it is double in bulk. Will take 90 to 120 minutes to rise.

When dough has doubled, remove the dough and roll out between two pieces of parchment paper or you can stretch and pat it. Dough should be between ½ inch and ¾ inch thick, cut into 3-inch circles using a glass or a biscuit cutter. You should end up with 12 rolls. Place on Pam or greased cookie sheet, cover and let rise until double in bulk. Will take 90 to 120 minutes.

Filling:

8 oz. cream cheese (room temperature)
⅓ c. Splenda
1 egg
1 tsp. vanilla

Mix cream cheese, Splenda, egg and vanilla until well blended. After rolls have risen, make indentations about 1 inch wide in center of each ball, pressing to bottom. Fill each with 1 to 2 tablespoons cream cheese filling. Bake 8 to 10 minutes at 350° until light brown. Remove from oven and drizzle with a Glaze. See index for recipe.

Note: Total recipe: 77 carbohydrates, 8 fiber and 168 protein. Makes 12 servings.

PEACHY CREAM CINNAMON ROLLS

(Bread Machine Recommended)

Parchment paper
1 T. bread machine yeast
½ c. warm water (105°-115°)
1 tsp. sugar
⅓ c. heavy whipping cream
2 T. soft butter
1 egg
2 T. Splenda
1 c. Vital wheat gluten flour
½ c. oat flour
½ c. vanilla whey protein powder
1 tsp. xanthan gum
1 tsp. cinnamon

Use your bread machine with these ingredients. Follow the manufacturer's directions for the order you add ingredients. Set the machine for dough cycle.

If not using the bread machine, sprinkle the yeast and sugar in warm water, stir and let it set for a few minutes. Yeast should bubble. If it doesn't then it may be out of date or your water temperature is wrong. In a bowl, mix cream, butter, eggs and yeast together. Add Splenda, Vital wheat gluten flour, oat flour, vanilla whey protein powder, xanthan gum and cinnamon. Mix at slow speed for 3 minutes. Scrape from sides of bowl and form the best ball you can as dough will be sticky. Cover and put in a warm place until it is double in bulk. (Turn the oven to its lowest degree while I prepare the dough and then turn it off and place covered dough in the oven to rise.) Will take 90 to 120 minutes to rise. If you wish to make the rolls at a later time you may place covered dough in refrigerator. When you remove the dough, you will then let it rise until it is double in bulk. Will take 90 to 120 minutes to rise. If you wish to make the rolls at a later time you may place covered dough in refrigerator. When you remove the dough, you will then let it rise until it is double in bulk. Will take 90 to 120 minutes to rise.

When dough has doubled, remove the dough and roll out between two pieces of parchment paper in a rectangle shape, approximately 12 x 10 inches.

Filling:

4 oz. cream cheese (room temperature)
1 sm. (4-oz.) jar peach baby food
1 T. Sugar Twin Spoonable brown sugar
¼ tsp. cinnamon
2 tsp. Splenda

Spread dough with 4 ounces of cream cheese that has been softened to room temperature. On top of the cream cheese spread 1 small (4-ounce) jar of peach baby food. Mix together 1 tablespoon of Sugar Twin Spoonable brown sugar, ¼ teaspoon cinnamon and 1 teaspoon of Splenda. Spread over cream cheese. Roll rectangle up tightly, beginning at 22-inch side. Pinch edges of dough into roll to seal. Stretch and shape until even. Cut roll into 12 pieces. Place slightly apart in buttered 9 x 12-inch pan. Brush with melted butter and let rise 90 to 120 minutes until again double in bulk. Bake at 350° oven for 10 to 15 minutes until lightly brown. Remove from oven and immediately invert pan on a sheet of wax paper. Serve warm.

Note: Total recipe is 86 carbohydrates, 10 fiber and 155 protein. Makes 12 servings.

38656-01

MACADAMIA COCONUT HORSESHOE

(Bread Machine Recommended)

Parchment paper
1 T. bread machine yeast
½ c. warm water (105°-115°)
1 tsp. sugar
⅓ c. heavy whipping cream
2 T. soft butter
1 egg
2 T. Sugar Twin Spoonable brown sugar
1 c. Vital wheat gluten flour
½ c. oat flour
½ c. vanilla whey protein powder
1 tsp. xanthan gum

Use your bread machine with these ingredients. Follow the manufacturer's for the order you add ingredients. Set the machine for dough cycle.

If not using the bread machine, sprinkle the yeast and sugar in warm water, stir and let it set for a few minutes. Yeast should bubble. If it doesn't, then it may be out of date or your water temperature is wrong. In a bowl, mix cream, butter, egg and yeast together. Add Sugar Twin Spoonable brown sugar, Vital wheat gluten flour, oat flour, vanilla whey protein powder and xanthan gum. Mix at slow speed for 3 minutes. Scrape from sides of bowl and form the best ball you can as dough will be sticky. Cover and put in a warm place until it is double in bulk. (I turn the oven to its lowest degree while I prepare the dough and then turn it off and place covered dough in the oven to rise.) Will take 90 to 120 minutes to rise. If you wish to make the rolls at a layer time you may place covered dough in refrigerator. When you remove the dough you will then let it rise until it is double in bulk. Will take 90 to 120 minutes to rise.

When dough has doubled, remove the dough and roll out between two pieces of parchment paper in a rectangle shape, approximately 12 x 10 inches.

Filling;

¼ c. butter
2 T. Splenda
2 T. Sugar Twin Spoonable brown sugar
⅓ c. unsweetened coconut
½ c. finely chopped macadamia nuts

Melt butter and brush on rolled out dough combine 2 tablespoons Splenda, 2 tablespoons Sugar Twin Spoonable brown sugar and ⅓ cup coconut. Sprinkle over buttered dough. Sprinkle with nuts. Roll rectangle up tightly, beginning at 12-inch size. Shape roll into horseshoe shape on a greased cookie sheet. With a sharp knife or kitchen shears, make cuts 1 inch apart around the outside edge of horseshoe, cutting through to ½ inch of center. Twist cut sections almost flat so that the filling shows. Brush with melted butter and let rise 90 to 120 minutes until again double in bulk. Bake at 350° for 15 to 20 minutes until light brown.

Note: Total recipe is 81 carbohydrates, 10 fiber, 153 protein without Glaze. Prepare a Glaze and dribble over ring. See index for recipes. Makes 12 servings.

ORANGE NUT HORSESHOE

(Bread Machine Recommended)

Parchment paper
1 T. bread machine yeast
½ c. warm water (105°-115°)
1 tsp. sugar
⅓ c. heavy whipping cream
2 T. soft butter
1 egg
2 T. Splenda
1 c. Vital wheat gluten flour
½ c. oat flour
½ c. vanilla whey protein powder
1 tsp. xanthan gum
1 tsp. cinnamon
1 tsp. orange peel

Use your bread machine with these ingredients. Follow the manufacturer's directions for the order you add ingredients Set the machine for dough cycle.

If not using the bread machine, sprinkle the yeast and sugar in warm water, stir and let it set for a few minutes. Yeast should bubble. If it doesn't, then it may be out of date or your water temperature is wrong. In a bowl, mix cream, butter, egg and yeast together. Add Splenda, Vital wheat gluten flour, oat flour, vanilla whey protein powder xanthan gum, cinnamon and orange peel. Mix at low speed for 3 minutes. Scrape from sides of bowl and from the best ball you can as dough will be sticky. Cover and put in a warm place until it is double in bulk. (It turn the oven to its lowest degree while I prepare the dough and then turn it off and place covered dough in the oven to rise.) Will take 90 to 120 minutes to rise. If you wish to make the rolls at a later time you may place covered dough in refrigerator. When you remove the dough, you will then let it rise until it is double in bulk. Will take 90 to 120 minutes to rise.

When dough has doubled, remove the dough and roll out between two pieces of parchment paper in a rectangle shape, approximately 12 x 10 inches.

Filling:

¼ c. butter
¼ c. Splenda
¼ tsp. cinnamon
¼ tsp. pkg. Kool-Aid orange drink
¼ c. finely chopped walnuts

Melt butter and brush on rolled out dough. Combine ¼ cup Splenda, ¼ teaspoon cinnamon and ¼ teaspoon of package of Kool-Aid orange drink. Sprinkle over buttered dough. Sprinkle with nuts. Roll rectangle up tightly, beginning at 12-inch side. Shape roll into horseshoe shape on a greased cookie sheet. With a sharp knife or kitchen shears, make cuts 1 inch apart around the outside edge of horseshoe cutting through to ½ inch of center. Twist cut sections almost flat o that the filling shows. Brush with melted butter and let rise 90 to 120 minutes until again double in bulk. Bake at 350° oven for 15 to 20 minutes until light brown.

Note: Total recipe is 83 carbohydrates, 12 fiber, 150 protein without Glaze. Prepare a Glaze and dribble over ring. See index for recipe. Makes 12 servings.

38656-01

PECAN HORSESHOE

(Bread Machine Recommended)

Parchment paper
1 T. bread machine yeast
½ c. warm water (105°-115°)
1 tsp. sugar
⅓ c. heavy whipping cream
2 T. soft butter
1 egg
2 T. Splenda
1 c. Vital wheat gluten flour
½ c. oat flour
½ c. vanilla whey protein powder
1 tsp. xanthan gum
1 tsp. cinnamon

Use your bread machine with these ingredients. Follow the manufacturer's directions for the order you add ingredients. Set the machine for dough cycle.

If not using the bread machine, sprinkle the yeast and sugar in warm water, stir and let it set for a few minutes. Yeast should bubble. If it t doesn't then it may be out of date or your water temperature is wrong. In a bowl, mix cream, butter, egg and yeast together. Add Splenda, Vital wheat gluten flour, oat flour, vanilla whey protein powder xanthan gum and cinnamon. Mix at slow speed for 3 minutes. Scrape from sides of bowl and form the best ball you can as dough will be sticky. Cover and put in a warm place until it is double in bulk. (I turn the oven to its lowest degree while I prepare the dough and then turn it off and place covered dough in the oven to rise.) Will take 90 to 120 minutes to rise. If you wish to make the rolls at a later time you may place covered dough in refrigerator. When you remove the dough, you will then let it rise until it is double in bulk. Will take 90 to 120 minutes to rise.

When dough has doubled, remove the dough and roll out between two pieces of parchment paper in a rectangle shape, approximately 12 x 10 inches.

Filling:

¼ c. butter
2 T. Splenda
½ tsp. cinnamon
1 T. Sugar Twin Spoonable brown sugar
½ c. finely chopped pecans

Melt butter and brush on rolled out dough. Combine 2 tablespoons Splenda, ¼ teaspoon cinnamon and 1 tablespoon Sugar Twin brown sugar. Sprinkle over buttered dough. Sprinkle with nuts. Roll rectangle up tightly, beginning at 12-inch side. Shape roll into horseshoe shape on a greased cookie sheet. With a sharp knife or kitchen shears, make cuts 1 inch apart around the outside edge of horseshoe, cutting through to ½ inch of center. Twist cut sections almost flat so that the filling shows. Brush with melted butter and let rise 90 to 120 minutes until again double in bulk. Bake at 350° oven for 15 to 20 minutes until light brown.

Note: Total recipe is 84 carbohydrates, 09 fiber, 150 protein without Glaze. Prepare a Glaze and dribble over rings. See index for recipe. Makes 12 servings.

38656-01

Quick Breads

Breads, Muffins, Pizza Dough, Coffee Cakes, Loaves, Crackers, Popovers, Scones, Donuts, Fritters & Funnel Cakes

My Favorite Recipe

QUICK BREADS

BISCUITS

1 c. natural whey protein powder
1 c. Vital wheat gluten flour
1 T. baking powder
½ tsp. baking soda
½ tsp. salt
½ c. shortening
¼ c. cream mixed with ¼ c. water (total ½ c.)

Whisk together whey protein, gluten flour, baking powder, baking soda and salt; mix well. With pastry blender or two knives cut shortening into dry ingredients until mixture is size of peas. Add cream mixture and stir well. Dough should stick together. If it doesn't, add 1 teaspoon of water at a time. Dough will be sticky. Put dough between two pieces or parchment paper. With a rolling pin, roll to approximately ½ to ¾ inch thick. Use a biscuit cutter of small glass to cut out your biscuits. Put on a cookie sheet about 1 inch apart or touching for soft sides. Bake at 350° for 5 to 8 minutes, until light brown on the bottom. Makes around 12 biscuits. You can brush with melted butter when they come out if you want a soft top.

Note: Total recipe: 36 carbohydrates, 2 fiber and 173 protein.

CHEESE BISCUITS

1 c. natural whey protein powder
1 c. Vital wheat gluten flour
1 T. baking powder
½ tsp. baking soda
½ c. shortening
¼ c. cream mixed with ¼ cup water (total ½ c.)
½ c. cheddar cheese, shredded
¼ c. melted butter
¼ tsp. garlic powder

Whisk together whey protein, gluten flour, baking powder and baking soda; mix well. With pastry blender or two knives cut shortening into dry ingredients until mixture is size of peas. Add cream mixture and cheese; stir well. Dough should stick together. If it doesn't, add 1 teaspoon of water at time. Dough will be sticky. Put dough between two pieces of parchment paper. With a rolling pin, roll to approximately ½ to ¾ inch thick. Use a biscuit cutter of small glass to cut out your biscuits. Put on a cookie sheet about 1 inch apart or touching for soft sides. Bake at 350° for 5 to 8 minutes, until light brown on the bottom. Makes around 12 biscuits. Melt butter and add garlic and brush with melted butter when they come out.

Note: Total recipe: 37 carbohydrates, 2 fiber and 184 protein.

38656-01

COTTAGE CHEESE BISCUITS

1¼ c. natural whey protein powder
1 c. Vital wheat gluten flour
1 T. baking powder
½ tsp. baking soda
½ tsp. salt
½ c. shortening
1 egg
½ c. cottage cheese

Whisk together whey protein, gluten flour, baking powder, baking soda and salt; mix well. With pastry blender or two knives, cut shortening into dry ingredients until mixture is size of peas. Add cottage cheese and stir well. Dough should stick together. If it doesn't, add 1 teaspoon of water at a time. Dough will be sticky. Put dough between two pieces of parchment paper. With a rolling pin, roll to approximately ½ to ¾ inch thick. Use a biscuits cutter of small glass to cut out your biscuits. Put on a cookie sheet about 1 inch apart of touching for soft sides. Bake at 350° for 5 to 8 minutes, until light brown on the bottom. Makes around 12 biscuits. You can brush with melted butter when they come out if you want a soft top.

Note: Total recipe: 36 carbohydrate, 2 fiber and 173 protein.

SOUR CREAM BISCUITS

1 c. natural whey protein powder
1 c. Viral wheat gluten flour
1 T. baking powder
½ tsp. baking soda
½ tsp. salt
½ c. shortening
¼ c. sour cream
¼ c. water

Whisk together whey protein, gluten flour, baking powder, baking soda and salt; mix well. With pastry blender or two knives cut shortening into dry ingredients until mixture is size of peas. Combine sour cream and water; add to dry ingredients. Dough should stick together. If it doesn't, add 1 teaspoon of water at a time. Dough will be sticky. Put dough between two pieces of parchment paper. With a rolling pin, roll to approximately ½ to ¾ inch thick. Use a biscuit cutter of small glass to cut out your biscuits. Put on a cookie sheet about 1 inch apart or touching for soft sides. Bake at 350° for 5 to 8 minutes until light brown on the bottom. Makes around 12 biscuits. You can brush with melted butter when they come out if you want a soft top.

Note: Total recipe: 36 carbohydrates, 2 fiber and 173 protein.

38656-01

SWEET DROP BISCUITS/SHORTCAKE

1 c. vanilla whey protein
½ c. Vital wheat gluten flour
½ c. oat flour
1 T. baking powder
½ tsp. baking soda
½ tsp. salt
3 T. Splenda
½ c. shortening
½ c. cream mixed with ¼ cup water (total ¾ c.)

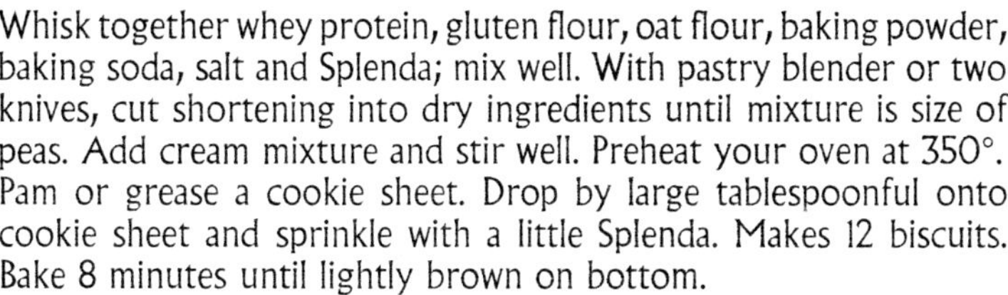

Whisk together whey protein, gluten flour, oat flour, baking powder, baking soda, salt and Splenda; mix well. With pastry blender or two knives, cut shortening into dry ingredients until mixture is size of peas. Add cream mixture and stir well. Preheat your oven at 350°. Pam or grease a cookie sheet. Drop by large tablespoonful onto cookie sheet and sprinkle with a little Splenda. Makes 12 biscuits. Bake 8 minutes until lightly brown on bottom.

Note: Total recipe is 57 carbohydrates, 5 fiber and 134 protein.

APPLE BRAN MUFFINS

½ c. hot water
1 pkg. Alpine sugar-free spiced cider instant apple-flavor drink mix
¾ c. All-Bran extra fiber cereal
⅔ c. oil
⅓ c. heavy whipping cream
2 eggs
1 tsp. molasses
1 T. Splenda
1 c. vanilla whey protein powder
1 T. oats flour
2 T. Vital wheat gluten flour
1½ tsp. baking powder
½ tsp. soda
1 tsp. cinnamon

Mix apple cider into hot water and pour over All-Bran. Allow to soak for 10 minutes. Then, add oil, whipping cream, eggs, molasses and Splenda and mix. Combine protein powder, oat flour, Vital wheat gluten flour, baking powder, soda and cinnamon; mix into the liquid ingredients. Pour into 12 Pam sprayed muffin cups. Bake at 350° for 10 to 15 minutes. Keep an eye on them to they don't overcook.

Note: Total recipe: 44 carbohydrates, 13 fiber and 109 protein.

38656-01

BANANA CHOCOLATE CHIP MUFFINS

½ c. water
⅔ c. oil
⅓ c. heavy whipping cream
3 eggs
1 sm. (2.5-oz.) jar baby food, bananas
1 tsp. banana extract
2 tsp. liquid sweetener Sweet 'N Low
3 T. Splenda
1¼ c. vanilla whey protein powder
2 T. oat flour
2 T. Vital wheat gluten flour
1½ tsp. xanthan gum
2 tsp. baking powder
½ c. mini chocolate chips

Combine water, oil, whipping cream, eggs, bananas, vanilla and liquid sweetener; mix. Add Splenda, vanilla, whey protein powder, oat flour, gluten flour, xanthan gum and baking powder; mix until moistened. Stir in chocolate chips. Pour into 12 Pam sprayed muffin cups. Bake at 350° for 10 to 15 minutes. Keep an eye on them so they don't overcook.

Note: Total recipe: 123 carbohydrates, 10 fiber and 137 protein.

BANANA PEANUT BUTTER MUFFINS

⅓ c. heavy whipping cream
¾ c. water
⅓ c. oil
2 eggs
1 sm. (2.5-oz.) jar baby food bananas
¼ c. unsweetened peanut butter
2 T. Splenda
1¼ c. vanilla whey protein powder
2 T. oat flour
2 tsp. xanthan gum
2 tsp. baking powder
½ tsp. salt
2 T. Vital wheat gluten flour

Combine whipping cream, water, oil, eggs, bananas and peanut butter; mix. Add Splenda, whey powder, oat flour, xanthan gum, baking powder, salt and gluten flour. Stir in nuts. Pour into 12 Pam-sprayed muffin cups. Bake at 350° for 10 to 15 minutes. Keep an eye on them so they don't overcook.

Note: Total recipe: 60 carbohydrates, 12 fiber and 144 protein.

38656-01

BANANA WALNUT MUFFINS

1/3 c. heavy whipped cream
3/4 c. water
2/3 c. oil
2 eggs
2 sm. (2.5-oz.) jar baby food bananas
2 T. Splenda
1 1/4 c. vanilla whey protein powder
2 T. oat flour
2 tsp. xanthan gum
2 tsp. baking powder
1/2 tsp. salt
2 T. Vital wheat gluten flour
1/2 tsp. cinnamon
1/4 c. chopped walnuts

Combine whipping cream, water, oil, eggs and bananas; mix. Add Splenda, whey powder, oat flour, xanthan gum, baking powder, salt, gluten, flour and cinnamon. Stir in nuts. Pour into 12 Pam-sprayed muffin cups. Bake at 350° for 10 to 15 minutes. Keep an eye on them so they don't overcook.

Note: Total recipe 71 carbohydrates, 12 fiber and 132 protein.

BRAN MUFFINS

2/3 c. oil
3/4 c. water
1 1/3 c. heavy whipping cream
2 eggs
1 tsp. vanilla extract
1 tsp. molasses
2 T. Splenda
1 1/4 c. vanilla whey protein powder
2 T. oat flour
2 T. Vital wheat gluten flour
2 tsp. baking powder
2 tsp. xanthan gum
1/2 c. toasted wheat bran
1/4 c. chopped walnuts

Combine oil, water, whipping cream, eggs, vanilla and molasses; mix. Add Splenda, vanilla, whey protein powder, oat flour, gluten flour, baking powder, xanthan gum and wheat bran; mix until moistened. Stir in nuts. Pour into 12 Pam-sprayed muffin cups. Bake at 350° for 10 to 15 minutes. Keep an eye on them so they don't overcook.

Note: Total recipe: 48 carbohydrates, 12 fiber and 132 protein.

BLUEBERRY MUFFINS

½ c. water
⅔ c. oil
⅓ c. heavy whipping cream
3 eggs
2 tsp. liquid sweetener Sweet 'N Low
3 T. Splenda
1¼ c. vanilla whey protein powder
2 T. oat flour
2 T. Vital wheat gluten flour
2 tsp. xanthan gum
2 tsp. baking powder
1 c. fresh blueberries

Wash blueberries and let them drain while you prepare batter. Combine water, oil whipping cream, eggs and liquid sweetener; mix. Add Splenda, vanilla, whey protein powder, oat flour, gluten flour, xanthan gum and baking powder; mix until moistened. Fold in blueberries. Pour into 12 Pam-sprayed muffin cups. Bake at 350° for 10 to 15 minutes. Keep an eye on them so they don't overcook.

Note: Total recipe: 56 carbohydrates, 13 fiber and 134 protein.

CARROT MUFFINS

⅓ c. heavy whipping cream
¾ c. water
⅔ c. oil
2 eggs
1 sm. (4-oz.) jar baby food carrots
2 tsp. liquid sweetener Sweet 'N Low
3 T. Splenda
1¼ c. vanilla whey protein powder
2 T. oat flour
2 tsp. xanthan gum
2 tsp. baking powder
½ tsp. salt
2 T. Vital wheat gluten flour
½ tsp. nutmeg
1 tsp. cinnamon
¼ c. chopped nuts

Combine whipping cream, water, oil, eggs, carrots and Sweet 'N Low; mix. Add Splenda, whey protein powder, oat flour, xanthan gum, baking powder, salt, wheat gluten flour, nutmeg and cinnamon. Stir in nuts. Pour into 12 Pam-sprayed muffin cups. Bake at 350° for 10 to 15 minutes. Keep an eye on then so they don't overcook.

Note: Total recipe: 48 carbohydrates, 12 fiber and 132 protein.

38656-01

CHOCOLATE WHISKEY MUFFINS

½ c. water
1 T. whiskey
⅔ c. oil
⅓ c. heavy whipping cream
3 eggs
1 tsp. vanilla extract
2 tsp. liquid sweetener Sweet 'N Low
3 T. Splenda
1¼ c. vanilla whey protein powder
2 T. oat flour
2 T. Vital wheat gluten flour
1½ tsp. xanthan gum
¼ c. baking cocoa
2 tsp. baking powder
½ c. chopped almonds

Combine water, whiskey, oil, whipping cream, eggs, vanilla and liquid sweetener; mix. Add Splenda, vanilla whey protein powder, oat flour, gluten flour, xanthan gum, baking cocoa and baking powder; mix until moistened. Stir in nuts. Pour into 12 Pam-sprayed muffin cups. Bake at 350° for 10 to 15 minutes. Keep an eye on them so they don't overcook.

Note: Total recipe: 61 carbohydrates, 16 fiber and 151 protein.

FLAX MUFFINS

¾ c. water
⅔ c. oil
⅓ c. heavy whipping cream
3 eggs
1 tsp. lemon extract
2 tsp. liquid sweetener Sweet 'N Low
3 T. Splenda
1¼ c. vanilla whey protein powder
2 T. oat flour
2 T. Vital wheat gluten flour
1½ tsp. xanthan gum
2 tsp. baking powder
½ c. ground flax seed

Combine water, oil, whipping cream, eggs, lemon and liquid sweetener; mix. Add Splenda, vanilla whey protein powder, oat flour, gluten flour, xanthan gum and baking powder; mix until moistened. Stir in flax seeds. Pour into 12 Pam-sprayed muffin cups. Bake at 350° for 10 to 15 minutes. Keep an eye on them so they don't overcook.

Note: Total recipe: 45 carbohydrates, 15 fiber and 139 protein.

38656-01

HEALTHY MUFFINS

½ c. water
⅔ c. oil
⅓ c. heavy whipping cream
3 eggs
1 tsp. vanilla extract
1 tsp. molasses
1 tsp. cinnamon
3 T. Splenda
1¼ c. vanilla whey protein powder
2 T. oat flour
2 T. Vital wheat gluten flour
1½ tsp. xanthan gum
2 tsp. baking powder
3 T. sunflower seed kernels
3 T. flax seed, ground
3 T. chopped almonds
¼ c. unsweetened coconut

Combine water, oil, whipping cream, eggs, vanilla and molasses; mix. Add cinnamon, Splenda, vanilla whey protein powder, oat flour, gluten flour, xanthan gum and baking powder; mix until moistened. Stir in sunflower kernels, flax seed, almonds and coconut. Pour into 12 Pam-sprayed muffin cups. Bake at 350° for 10 to 15 minutes. Keep an eye on them so they don't overcook.

Note: Total recipe: 57 carbohydrates, 18 fiber and 147 protein.

MOCHA MUFFINS

2 tsp. instant coffee
½ c. hot water
⅔ c. oil
½ c. heavy whipping cream
3 eggs
1 tsp. vanilla extract
2 tsp. liquid sweetener Sweet 'N Low
2 T. baking cocoa
3 T. Splenda
1¼ c. vanilla whey protein powder
2 T. oat flour
2 T. Vital wheat gluten flour
1½ tsp. xanthan gum
½ tsp. baking soda
2 tsp. baking powder

Stir coffee into hot water. Combine water, oil, whipping cream, eggs, vanilla and liquid sweetener; mix. Add cocoa, Splenda, vanilla whey protein powder, oat flour, gluten flour, xanthan gum and baking powder; mix until moistened. Pour into 12 Pam-sprayed muffin cups. Bake at 350° for 10 to 15 minutes. Keep an eye on them so they don't overcook.

Note; Total recipe: 42 carbohydrates, 9 fiber and 136 protein.

38656-01

ORANGE CARROT MUFFINS

½ c. water
⅔ c. oil
⅓ c. heavy whipping cream
2 eggs
1 sm. (4-oz.) jar baby food carrots
1½ tsp. orange extract
2 tsp. liquid sweetener Sweet 'N Low
3 T. Splenda
1¼ c. vanilla whey protein powder
2 T. oat flour
2 T. Vital wheat gluten flour
1½ tsp. xanthan gum
2 tsp. orange peel
2 tsp. cinnamon
½ tsp. ginger
1 tsp. baking soda
2 tsp. baking powder

Combine water, oil, whipping cream, eggs, carrots, orange extract and liquid sweetener; mix. Add Splenda, vanilla whey protein powder, oat flour, gluten flour, xanthan gum, orange peel, cinnamon, ginger, baking soda and baking powder; mix until moistened. Pour into 12 Pam-sprayed muffin cups. Bake at 350° for 10 to 15 minutes. Keep an eye on them so they don't overcook.

Note: Total recipe: 49 carbohydrates, 11 fiber and 128 protein.

POPPY SEED MUFFINS

½ c. water
⅔ c. oil
⅓ c. heavy whipping cream
3 eggs
1 tsp. lemon extract
2 tsp. liquid sweetener Sweet 'N Low
3 T. Splenda
1¼ c. vanilla whey protein powder
2 T. oat flour
2 T. Vital wheat gluten flour
1½ tsp. xanthan gum
2 tsp. baking powder
1 T. poppy seeds

Combine water, oil, whipping cream, eggs, lemon and liquid sweetener; mix. Add Splenda, vanilla whey protein powder, oat flour, gluten flour, xanthan gum and baking powder; mix until moistened. Stir in poppy seeds. Pour into 12 Pam-sprayed muffin cups. Bake at 350° for 10 to 15 minutes. Keep an eye on them so they don't overcook.

Note: Total recipe: 35 carbohydrates, 9 fiber and 135 protein.

38656-01

RASPBERRY MUFFINS

½ c. water
⅔ c. oil
⅓ c. heavy whipping cream
3 eggs
½ tsp. lemon extract
2 tsp. liquid sweetener Sweet 'N Low
3 T. Splenda
1¼ c. vanilla whey protein powder
2 T. oat flour
2 T. Vital wheat gluten flour
1½ tsp. xanthan gum
1 T. baking powder
1 c. fresh raspberries

Rinse and drain raspberries while your prepare batter. Combine water, oil, whipping cream, eggs, vanilla and liquid sweetener; mix. Add Splenda, vanilla whey protein powder, oat flour, gluten flour, xanthan gum and baking powder; mix until moistened. Fold in raspberries. Pour into 12 Pam-sprayed muffin cups. Bake at 350° for 10 to 15 minutes. Keep an eye on them so they don't overcook.

Note: Total recipe: 49 carbohydrates, 17 fiber and 134 protein.

RHUBARB MUFFINS

1 c. diced rhubarb
½ c. water
⅔ c. oil
⅓ c. heavy whipping cream
3 eggs
1 tsp. vanilla extract
1 tsp. molasses
3 T. Splenda
1¼ c. vanilla whey protein powder
2 T. oat flour
2 T. Vital wheat gluten flour
1½ tsp. xanthan gum
½ tsp. cinnamon
½ tsp. baking soda
2 tsp. baking powder

Combine rhubarb, water, oil, whipping cream, eggs, vanilla and molasses; mix. Add Splenda, vanilla whey protein powder, oat flour, gluten flour, xanthan gum, cinnamon, baking soda and baking powder; mix until moistened. Pour into 12 Pam-sprayed muffin cups. Bake at 350° for 10 to 15 minutes. Keep an eye on them so they don't overcook.

Note: Total recipe: 46 carbohydrates, 11 fiber and 135 protein.

38656-01

SWEET POTATO MUFFINS

1 sm. (2½-oz.) jar baby food sweet potatoes
⅔ c. oil
2 eggs
⅓ c. whipping cream
¾ c. water
1 tsp. molasses
½ c. chopped walnuts
1¼ c. vanilla whey protein powder
2 T. Vital wheat gluten flour
2 T. oat flour
2 tsp. xanthan gum
2 tsp. baking powder
¼ tsp. ground ginger
⅛ tsp. ground cloves
1 tsp. salt
1 tsp. cinnamon

Combine sweet potatoes, oil, eggs, whipping cream and water; mix. Add molasses, walnuts, whey powder, gluten flour, oat flour, xanthan gum, baking powder, baking soda, salt, ginger, cloves and cinnamon. Stir in nuts. Pour into 12 Pam-sprayed muffin cups. Bake at 350° for 10 to 15 minutes. Keep an eye on them so they don't overcook.

Note: Total recipe: 60 carbohydrates, 12 fiber and 137 protein.

BLUEBERRY COFFEE CAKE

¼ c. water
¼ c. cream
½ c. oil
2 eggs
¼ c. Splenda
1 c. vanilla whey protein
2 T. Vital wheat gluten flour
¼ c. oat flour
1 T. baking powder
1 tsp. baking soda
½ c. chopped blueberries

Combine water, cream, oil, eggs, and Splenda; mix. Add whey protein, gluten flour, oat flour, baking powder and soda; mix well. Stir in blueberries. Pour into a greased 8-inch cake pan and prepare topping.

Topping:

¼ c. Splenda
1 T. oat flour
½ tsp. cinnamon
¼ c. butter

Splenda, oat flour, cinnamon and cut into the cold butter to make a crumbly topping. Sprinkle on top and bake 25 minutes at 375°. Sprinkle on top and bake for 25 minutes at 375°.

Note: Total recipe: 55 carbohydrates, 6 fiber, 108 protein.

38656-01

CHOCOLATE COFFEE CAKE

½ c. water
½ c. cream
½ c. oil
3 eggs
½ c. Splenda
1 c. vanilla whey protein
¼ c. baking cocoa
2 T. Vital wheat gluten flour
2 T. oat flour
1 tsp. baking powder
1 tsp. baking soda

Combine water, cream, oil, eggs and Splenda; mix. Add whey protein, baking cocoa, gluten flour, oat flour, baking powder and soda; mix well. Pour into a greased 8-inch cake pan and prepare topping:

Topping:

¼ c. chopped walnuts
¼ c. mini chocolate chips

Sprinkle on top and bake for 25 minutes at 375°.

Note: Total recipe: 85 carbohydrates, 8 fiber, 118 protein.

CHOCOLATE RIPPLE COFFEE CAKE

½ c. water
½ c. cream
½ c. oil
3 eggs
½ c. Splenda
1 c. vanilla whey protein
2 T. Vital wheat gluten flour
2 T. oat flour
1 tsp. baking powder
1 tsp. baking soda

Combine water, cream, oil, eggs and Splenda; mix. Add whey protein, gluten flour, oat flour, baking powder and soda; mix well. Pour into a greased 8-inch cake pan and prepare filling.

Filling:

2 T. chopped walnuts
2 T. Splenda
2 T. baking cocoa

Mix cocoa, Splenda and walnuts together. Spoon ½ of the batter into a greased 8-inch pan. Sprinkle half of the filling over the batter. Spoon rest of batter on top and sprinkle remaining filling. Bake at 375° for 25 minutes.

Note: Total recipe: 42 carbohydrates, 5 fiber, 116 protein.

38656-01

PEANUT BUTTER COFFEE CAKE

½ c. water
⅓ c. cream
2 T. oil
¼ c. unsweetened peanut butter
3 eggs
¼ c. Splenda
1 tsp. molasses
1 c. vanilla whey protein
2 T. Vital wheat gluten flour
2 T. oat flour
1 T. baking powder
1 tsp. baking soda

Combine water, cream, oil, peanut butter, eggs and Splenda; mix. Add whey protein, gluten flour, oat flour, baking powder and soda; mix well. Pour into a greased 8-inch cake and bake for 25 minutes. Sprinkle a little Splenda on top while warm.

Note: Total recipe: 48 carbohydrates, 6 fiber, 130 protein.

BANANA ORANGE LOAF

⅓ c. heavy whipped cream
¾ c. water
⅓ c. oil
2 eggs
2 sm. (2.5-oz.) jars baby food bananas
2 tsp. liquid sweetener Sweet 'N low
1 tsp. orange extract
3 T. Splenda
1½ c. vanilla whey protein powder
3 T. oat flour
2 tsp. xanthan gum
2 tsp. baking powder
½ tsp. salt
3 T. Vital wheat gluten flour
1 tsp. cinnamon
1 tsp. orange peel
¼ c. chopped nuts

Combine whipping cream, water, oil, eggs, bananas, Sweet 'N Low and extract; mix. Add Splenda, whey powder, oat flour, xanthan gum, baking powder, salt, Vital wheat gluten flour, cinnamon and orange peel. Stir in nuts. Pour into greased bread pan or line pan with parchment paper and bake at 350° for 40 to 45 minutes. Do not overbake.

Note: Total recipe: 79 carbohydrates, 12 fiber and 158 protein.

CARROT LOAF

1 sm. (4-oz.) jar baby food carrots
1/3 c. oil
2 eggs
1/3 c. whipping cream
3/4 c. water
1/3 c. Splenda
1/2 c. chopped walnuts
1 1/2 c. vanilla whey protein powder
3 T. Vital wheat gluten flour
1/3 c. oat flour
2 tsp. xanthan gum
2 tsp. baking powder
1 tsp. baking soda
1 tsp. nutmeg
1 tsp. salt
3 tsp. cinnamon

Combine carrots, oil, eggs, whipping cream and water; mix. Add Splenda, walnuts, whey powder, gluten flour, oat flour, xanthan gum, baking powder, baking soda, nutmeg, salt and cinnamon. Stir in nuts. Pour into greased bread pan or line pan with parchment paper and bake at 350° for 40 to 45 minutes. Do not overbake.

Note: Total recipe: 76 carbohydrates, 21 fiber and 164 protein.

CARROT ZUCCHINI LOAF

1 1/2 c. shredded, unpeeled zucchini
1 sm. (4-oz.) jar baby food carrots
2 eggs
1/2 c. oil
1/3 c. heavy whipping cream
1/4 c. water
1 tsp. molasses
1 tsp. orange extract
1 tsp. cinnamon
1/3 c. Splenda
1 1/2 c. vanilla whey protein powder
3 T. Vital wheat gluten flour
1/3 c. oat flour
1 tsp. xanthan gum
2 tsp. baking powder

Combine zucchini, carrots, eggs, oil, cream, water, molasses and orange extra; mix. Add cinnamon, Splenda, Whey protein powder, gluten flour, oat flour, xanthan gum and baking powder; mix until moistened. Pour into greased bread pan or line pan with parchment paper and bake at 350° for 40 to 45 minutes. Do not overbake.

Note: Total recipe: 59 carbohydrates, 12 fiber and 155 protein.

38656-01

CHOCOLATE ZUCCHINI LOAF

2 c. shredded, unpeeled zucchini
2 eggs
1/4 c. oil
1/3 c. unsweetened peanut butter
1/3 c. heavy whipping cream
1/4 c. water
1 T. liquid sweetener Sweet 'N Low
1/2 tsp. Watkins peanut butter extract
1/3 c. baking cocoa
1/2 c. Splenda
1 1/2 c. vanilla whey protein powder
3 T. Vital wheat gluten flour
1/4 c. oat flour
2 tsp. baking powder
1 tsp. xanthan gum

Combine zucchini, eggs, oil, peanut butter, cream, water, liquid sweetener and extract; mix. Add Splenda, vanilla whey protein, gluten flour, oat flour, baking powder and xanthan gum; mix until moistened. Pour into greased bread pan or line pan with parchment paper and bake at 350° for 40 to 45 minutes. Do not overbake.

Note: Total recipe: 75 carbohydrates, 14 fiber and 186 protein.

CRANBERRY LOAF

3/4 c. finely chopped fresh cranberries
2 eggs
1/2 c. oil
1/3 c. heavy whipping cream
1/2 c. water
2/3 c. Splenda
1 1/2 c. vanilla whey protein powder
3 T. Vital wheat gluten flour
1/3 c. oat flour
2 T. grated orange peel
2 tsp. baking powder
1 tsp. baking soda
1 tsp. salt
1/2 c. chopped walnuts

Combine cranberries, eggs, oil, cream, water and Splenda; mix. Add whey protein, gluten flour oat flour, baking powder, baking soda, salt, orange peel, nuts and mix until moistened. Pour into greased bread pan or line pan with parchment paper and bake at 350° for 40 to 45 minutes. Do not overbake.

Note: Total recipe: 64 carbohydrates, 11 fiber and 163 protein.

STRAWBERRY RHUBARB LOAF

1½ c. diced rhubarb
¾ c. strawberries
2 eggs
½ c. oil
⅓ c. heavy whipping cream
¼ c. water
1 T. liquid sweetener Sweet 'N Low
2 tsp. cinnamon
⅓ c. Splenda
1½ c. vanilla whey protein powder
3 T. Vital wheat gluten flour
⅓ c. oat flour
1 tsp. xanthan gum
2 tsp. baking powder
1 tsp. baking soda

Combine rhubarb, strawberries, eggs, oil, cream, water and sweetener; mix. Add cinnamon, Splenda, whey protein powder, gluten flour, oat flour, xanthan gum, baking powder and baking soda; mix until moistened. Pour into greased bread pan or line pan with parchment paper and bake at 350° for 40 to 45 minutes. Do not overbake.

Note: Total recipe: 55 carbohydrates, 13 fiber and 155 protein.

SWEET BRAN LOAF

⅔ c. oil
1¼ c. water
¼ c. heavy whipping cream
2 eggs
1 tsp. molasses
2 T. Splenda
1½ c. vanilla whey protein powder
2 T. oat flour
3 T. Vital wheat gluten flour
½ c. toasted wheat bran
2 tsp. xanthan gum
½ tsp. salt
2 tsp. baking powder
¾ tsp. cinnamon

Combine oil, water, heavy cream, eggs and molasses. Combine Splenda, vanilla whey protein, oat flour, Vital wheat gluten flour, wheat bran, xanthan gum, salt, baking powder and cinnamon. Add to liquid mixture and mix until moistened. Pour into greased bread pan or line pan with parchment paper and bake at 350° for 40 to 45 minutes. Do not overbake.

Note: Total recipe: 58 carbohydrates, 18 fiber and 155 protein.

38656-01

SWEET POTATO LOAF

1 sm. (2½-oz.) jar baby food sweet potatoes
½ c. oil
2 eggs
⅓ c. whipping cream
¾ c. water
1 tsp. molasses
½ c. chopped walnuts
1½ c. vanilla whey protein powder
3 T. Vital wheat gluten flour
⅓ c. oat flour
2 tsp. xanthan gum
2 tsp. baking powder
1 tsp. baking soda
½ tsp. ground ginger
⅛ tsp. ground cloves
1 tsp. salt
3 tsp. cinnamon

Combine sweet potatoes, oil, eggs, whipping cream and water; mix. Add molasses, walnuts, whey powder, gluten flour, oat flour, xanthan gum, baking powder, baking soda, ginger, cloves, salt and cinnamon. Stir in nuts. Pour into greased bread pan or line pan with parchment paper and bake at 350° for 40 to 45 minutes. Do not overbake.

Note: Total recipe: 85 carbohydrates, 20 fiber and 164 protein.

CARAWAY RYE CRACKERS

Parchment paper
¼ c. rye flour
1 c. natural whey protein powder
2 tsp. caraway seed
1 tsp. baking powder
½ tsp. baking soda
2 T. olive oil
2 T. cream
3 T. water

Whisk together rye flour, natural whey protein powder, caraway seed, baking powder and baking soda. Combine olive oil, cream, water and add to dry ingredients. Stir until forms a ball. If the dough doesn't stick together, add water a teaspoon at a time. Divide dough in half and with rolling pin, roll between two pieces of parchment paper. Roll thin. Slowly remove top paper and put dough with parchment paper on a cookie sheet. Score the dough in desired shapes and sizes. Bake at 350° for 5 to 6 minutes. Will be light brown on edges. Remove for oven and let cool until you can handle. Break or recut pieces. If you have some pieces that were too thick to crisp up, set aside until you are done with second half of dough. When you are done baking crackers, turn the oven off. Place uncrisp crackers on cookie sheet and place back in the oven with door cracked a little. Let oven cool and you should have crisp crackers. Store in airtight container. Room temperature.

Note: Total recipe: 33 carbohydrates, 7 fiber and 58 protein.

38656-01

CHEESE CRACKERS

Baking Low Carb Bread & Breakfast

Parchment paper
¼ c. wheat flour
1 c. natural whey protein powder
1 tsp. baking powder
½ tsp. baking soda
½ tsp. onion powder
1 T. olive oil
2 T. cream
3 T. water
⅓ c. grated cheese Cheddar, Swiss or Parmesan

Whisk together wheat flour, natural whey protein powder, baking powder and baking soda. Combine olive oil, cream, water, cheese and add to dry ingredients. Stir until forms a ball. If the dough doesn't stick together, add water a teaspoon at a time. Divide dough in half and with rolling pin, roll between two pieces of parchment paper. Roll thin. Slowly remove top paper and put dough with parchment paper on a cookie sheet. Score the dough in desired shapes and sizes. Salt lightly. Bake at 350° for 5 to 6 minutes. Will be light brown on edges. Remove from oven and let cool until you can handle. Break or recut pieces. If you have some pieces that were too thick to crisp up, set aside until you are done with second half of dough. When you are done baking crackers, turn the oven off. Place uncrisp crackers on cookie sheet and place back in the oven with door cracked a little. Let oven cool and you should have crisp crackers. Store in airtight container, room temperature.

Note: Total recipe: 36 carbohydrates, 5 fiber and 68 protein.

38656-01

CORN CRACKERS

Parchment paper
¼ c. wheat flour
1 c. natural whey protein powder
2 T. Vital wheat gluten flour
1 tsp. baking powder
1 tsp. salt
¼ c. puréed canned corn
2 T. olive oil
2 T. cream
3 T. water

Whisk together wheat flour, natural whey protein powder, gluten flour, baking powder, and salt. Combine puréed corn, olive oil, cream, water and add to dry ingredients. Stir until forms a ball. If the dough doesn't stick together, add water a teaspoon at a time. Divide dough in half and with rolling pin, roll between two pieces of parchment paper. Roll thin. Slowly remove top paper and put dough with parchment paper on a cookie sheet. Score the dough in desired shape and sizes. Salt lightly. Bake at 350° for 5 to 6 minutes. Will be light brown on edges. Remove from oven and let cool until you can handle. Break or recut pieces. If you have some pieces that were too thick to crisp up, set aside until you are done with second half of dough. When you are done baking crackers, turn the oven off. Place uncrisp crackers on cookie sheet and place back in the oven with door cracked a little. Let oven cool and you should have crisp crackers. Store in airtight container, room temperature.

Note: Total recipe: 45 carbohydrates 5 fiber and 71 protein.

38656-01

RYE-FLAVORED SEED FLATBREAD/CRACKERS

Barbara Pollack
Owner of Expert Foods

3 T. ThickenThin Not Starch thickener
5 T. sesame seeds (2 oz. by weight)
1 T. each poppy, caraway & slightly-crushed dill seed
¼ tsp. onion powder (opt.)
¼ tsp. salt or to taste
Pepper to taste
Up to 2 T. of any combination of finely-ground ground nuts, bran, flour, etc. (opt.)
½ c. water

Preheat oven to 400°. Cover the baking pan with parchment paper, foil or greased waxed paper (waxed paper is not really intended for oven use, but you can often get away with it). Combine dry ingredients. Stir in the water and spread evenly over the baking pan. Make sure the edges are at least as thick as the center, thicker is okay, as edges bake faster then the center. Bake at 400° for 20 to 25 minutes or until it's fairly dry and set or until the edges start to get brown. At this point, the center is likely to be bit damp, but it's also just minute away from developing an over-browned flavor. So turn down the oven (off, if the oven is well-insulated) and let it finish drying out. (If you want crackers, score it into sections at this time.) Once the top is dry, remove the parchment, if underside is damp, return it to the oven to dry out for a few minutes.

Note: 36.8 carbohydrates of which 28.4g fiber and could easily be cut into six or eight crackers. Needless to say, with that much fiber, don't overdo until you body is accustomed to it.

38656-01

ONION CRACKERS

Parchment paper
¼ c. wheat flour
1 c. natural whey protein powder
2 tsp. onion powder
1 tsp. baking powder
½ tsp. baking soda
½ tsp. onion powder
2 T. olive oil
2 T. cream
3 T. water

Whisk together wheat flour, natural whey protein powder, onion powder, baking powder and baking soda. Combine olive oil, cream, water and add to dry ingredients. Stir until forms a ball. If the dough doesn't stick together, add water a teaspoon at a time. Divide dough in half and with rolling pin. Roll between two pieces of parchment paper. Roll thin. Slowly remove top paper and put dough with parchment paper on a cookie sheet. Score the dough in desired shapes and sizes. Salt lightly. Bake at 350° for 5 to 6 minutes. Will be light brown on edges. Remove from oven and let cool until you can handle. Break or recut pieces. If you have some pieces that were too thick to crisp up, set aside until you are done with second half of dough. When you are done baking crackers, turn the oven off. Place uncrisp crackers on cookie sheet and place back in the oven with the door cracked a little. Let oven cool and you should have crisp crackers. Store in airtight container, room temperature.

Note: Total recipe: 35 carbohydrates, 5 fiber and 61 protein.

38656-01

POPPY SEED CRACKERS

Parchment paper
¼ c. wheat flour
1 c. natural whey protein powder
1 T. poppy seeds
1 tsp. baking powder
½ tsp. baking soda
½ tsp. onion powder
1 T. olive oil
2 T. cream
3 T. water

Whisk together wheat flour, natural whey protein powder, poppy seed, baking powder and baking soda. Combine olive oil, cream, water and add to dry ingredients. Stir until forms a ball. If the dough doesn't stick together, add water a teaspoon at a time. Divide dough in half and with rolling pin, roll between two pieces of parchment paper. Roll thin. Slowly remove top paper and put dough with parchment paper on a cookie sheet. Score the dough in desired, shapes and sizes. Bake at 350° for 5 to 6 minutes. Will be lightly brown on edges. Remove for oven and let cool until you can handle. Break or recut pieces. If you have some pieces that were too thick to crisp up, set aside until you are done with second half of the dough. when you are done baking crackers, turn the oven off. Place uncrisp crackers on cookie sheet and place back in the oven with door cracked a little. Let oven cool and you should have crisp crackers. Store in airtight container, room temperature.

Note: Total recipe: 34 carbohydrates, 8 fiber and 61 protein.

38656-01

SWEET CRACKERS

Parchment paper
¼ c. wheat flour
1 c. + 2 T. natural whey protein powder
1 tsp. cinnamon
1 tsp. baking powder
½ tsp. baking soda
3 T. Sugar Twin Spoonable brown sugar
2 T. Splenda
1 tsp. butter extract
1 tsp. molasses
2 T. olive oil
3 T. cream
3 T. water

Whisk together wheat flour, natural whey protein powder, cinnamon, baking powder, baking soda, Sugar Twin and Splenda. Combine butter extract, molasses, olive oil, cream, water and add to dry ingredients. Stir until forms a ball. If the dough doesn't stick together, add water a teaspoon at a time. Divide dough in half and with rolling pin, rolls between two pieces of parchment paper. Roll thin. Slowly remove top paper and put dough with parchment paper on a cookie sheet. Score the dough in desired shapes and sizes. Sprinkle lightly with Splenda. Bake at 350° for 5 to 6 minutes. Will be lightly brown on edges. Remove from oven and let cool until you can handle. Break or recut pieces. If you have some pieces that were to thick too crisp up, set aside until you are done with second half of dough. When you are done baking crackers, turn the oven off. Place uncrisp crackers on cookie sheet and place back in the oven with door cracked a little. Let oven cool and you should have crisp crackers. Store in airtight container, room temperature.

Note: Total recipe: 46 carbohydrates, 6 fiber and 59 protein.

SUNFLOWER PARMESAN CRACKERS

From Dana Carpteneter, Author
"How I gave Up My Low Fat Diet"

Parchment paper
1 c. raw hulled sunflower seeds
½ c. Parmesan cheese
¼ c. cold water

Preheat oven to 325°. In the food processor place 1 cup raw hulled sunflower seeds and ½ cup of Parmesan cheese and process until the mixture is a fine meal (about 30 seconds to a minute). Add ¼ cup cold water and process until well blended or it starts to roll up like pie dough. Turn the dough out on the parchment paper and tear off a sheet of parchment to use as a cover, either with your hands or lightly with a rolling pin, Press the dough into a thin sheet. Remove the top cover. The thinner the better. Score it with a knife into squares. Bake about 3 minutes or until lightly browned. Peel off parchment, break into square and cool thoroughly. Also as they cool, they crisp up wonderfully. Keep in tight container. The whole recipe has 29 carbohydrates, 15 fiber and 49 protein.

POPOVERS

¼ c. natural whey protein powder
½ c. Vital wheat gluten flour
¼ c. oat flour
½ tsp. salt
2 eggs
½ c. heavy cream
½ c. warm water

Whisk together whey protein, gluten flour, oat flour and salt; mix well. Whisk eggs until they are thoroughly mixed and change color. Add cream and water. Gently stir the wet ingredients into the dry ingredients; mix until only small lumps are left in it. Preheat the oven to 400°. Grease muffin tins well and spoon batter into 6 to 7 cups. Fill empty cups with water. Bake for 10 minutes at 450° ant then turn oven down to 350° and bake 10 to 15 minutes more until lightly brown. Remove from pan after a few minutes to keep from getting soggy. Serve warm or pierce each baked popover with the point of a knife to let the steam out and cool before storing in bag.

Note: Total recipe: 32 carbohydrates, 2 fiber and 77 protein.

SCONES

1 c. natural whey protein powder
1 c. Vital wheat gluten flour
1 T. baking powder
½ tsp. baking soda
½ tsp. salt
3 T. Splenda
½ c. shortening
3 T. cream mixed with 3 T. water & 1 slightly beaten egg

Whisk together whey protein, gluten flour, baking powder, baking soda, salt and Splenda; mix well. With pastry blend or two knives cut shortening into dry ingredients until mixture is size of peas. Add cream and egg mixture and stir well. Dough should stick together. If it doesn't, add 1 teaspoon of water at at time. Dough will be sticky. Put dough between two pieces of parchment paper. With a rolling pin, roll to approximately ¼ inch thick. Cut into triangle and diamond shapes. Put on a cookies sheet about 1 inch apart. Sprinkle lightly with Splenda. Bake at 350° for 5 to 8 minutes until light brown on the bottom.

Note: Total recipe: 37 carbohydrates, 2 fiber, 179 protein.

38656-01

PIZZA DOUGH

¼ c. wheat flour
1 c. natural whey protein powder
1 tsp. baking powder
½ tsp. garlic powder
1 tsp. butter extract
2 T. olive oil
2 T. cream
3 T. water

Whisk together wheat flour, natural whey protein powder, baking powder and garlic powder. Combine butter extract, olive oil, cream, water and add to dry ingredients. Stir until forms a ball. If the dough doesn't stick together, add water a teaspoon at a time. Put dough between two pieces of parchment paper. With rolling pin, roll to approximately a 14 x 10-inch rectangle. Slowly remove top paper and put dough with parchment paper on a cookie sheet. Top with your favorite pizza toppings. Bake at 350° for 10 to 20 minutes. Lift pizza with spatula to check for doneness when the edges are lightly brown. The heavier the topping, the longer it will take to bake.

Note: Total dough recipe: 35 carbohydrates, 5 fiber and 61 protein.

COCOA DONUT PUFFS

¾ c. Vital whey protein powder
¼ c. baking cocoa
1 c. Vital wheat gluten flour
1 T. baking powder
½ tsp. baking soda
½ tsp. salt
¼ tsp. nutmeg
½ tsp. cinnamon
¼ c. Splenda
1 egg
2 T. melted butter
¼ c. cream mixed with ¼ c. water (total ½ c.)

Preheat frying oil to 375°. Whisk together whey protein, baking cocoa, gluten flour, baking powder, baking soda, salt nutmeg, cinnamon and Splenda. Combine egg, butter, cream and water; stir into dry ingredients. Let dough rest for 5 minutes. Drop by spoonful into hot oil. Don't overload fryer, fry three to four at a time so they have room to float and turn. Cook to golden brown. If you wish you can toss in Splenda.

Note: Total recipe: 54 carbohydrates, 2 fiber, 163 protein.

38656-01

DONUT PUFFS

Baking Low Carb Bread & Breakfast

1 c. vanilla whey protein powder
1 c. Vital wheat gluten flour
1 T. baking powder
½ tsp. baking soda
½ tsp. salt
¼ tsp. nutmeg
½ tsp. cinnamon
¼ c. Splenda
1 egg
2 T. melted butter
¼ c. cream mixed with ¼ c. water (total ½ c.)

Preheat frying oil to 375°. Whisk together whey protein, gluten flour, baking powder, baking soda, salt, nutmeg, cinnamon and Splenda. Combine egg, butter and water; stir into dry ingredients. Let dough rest for 5 minutes. Drop by spoonful into hot oil. Don't overload fryer, fry three to four at a time so they have room to float and turn. Cook to golden brown. If you wish, you can toss in Splenda.

Note: Total recipe: 44 carbohydrates, 3 fiber, 180 protein.

APPLE FRITTERS

3 eggs
¼ c. hot water
1 pkg. Alpine sugar free spiced apple cider
1 T. heavy cream
2 T. oil
1 c. vanilla whey protein
1 T. baking powder
½ tsp. cinnamon
⅓ c. Splenda
1 T. xanthan gum

Preheat oven to 375°. Add cider to hot water to dissolve. Add to eggs, cream and oil; mix. Then mix in vanilla whey protein, baking powder, cinnamon, Splenda and xanthan gum. Drop by spoonful into hot oil. Don't overload fryer, fry three to four at a time so they have room to float and turn. Cook to golden brown. If you wish, you can let cool a little and toss in Splenda.

Note: Total recipe: 37 carbohydrates, 14 fiber, 99 protein.

38656-01

CINNAMON FRITTERS

- 2 eggs
- 3 T. water
- 2 T. heavy cream
- 3 T. oil
- 1 c. vanilla whey protein
- 1 T. baking powder
- 1 tsp. cinnamon
- ½ tsp. nutmeg
- ⅓ c. Splenda
- 1 tsp. xanthan gum

Preheat oil to 375°. Combine water, eggs, cream and oil; mix. Then mix in vanilla whey protein, baking powder, cinnamon, nutmeg, Splenda and xanthan gum. Drop by spoonful into hot oil. Don't overload, fry three to four at a time so they have room to float and turn. Cook to golden brown. If you wish, you can let cool a little and toss in Splenda.

Note: Total recipe: 33 carbohydrates, 15 fiber, 93 protein.

Quick Breads

ONION FRITTERS

- 3 eggs
- 2 T. water
- 2 T. heavy cream
- 3 T. oil
- 1 c. natural whey protein
- 1 T. baking powder
- 1 tsp. salt
- 1 T. dried onion
- 1 tsp. xanthan gum

Preheat oven to 375°. Combine eggs, water, cream and oil; mix. Whisk together whey protein, baking powder salt, dried onion and xanthan gum; mix into liquid ingredients until moistened. Drop by spoonful into hot oil. Don't over load fryer, fry three to four at a time so the have room to float and turn. Cook to golden brown.

Note: Total recipe: 23 carbohydrates, 6 fiber and 74 protein.

APPLE FUNNEL CAKES

- ¼ c. warm water
- 1 pkg. Alpine sugar free spiced apple cider
- 3 eggs
- 2 T. whipping cream
- 1 T. oil
- 1 c. vanilla whey protein
- 1 T. baking powder
- 1 tsp. baking soda
- ⅓ c. Splenda

Preheat oil to 375°. Mix apple cider into warm water and combine with eggs, cream and oil; mix. Then mix in vanilla whey protein, baking powder, baking soda, and Splenda pour mixture through a funnel going back and forth into hot oil. If too thick to go through funnel, add more water. Don't overload fryer so it has room to float. Cook to golden brown, Drain on paper towel. If you wish you can sprinkle with Splenda.

Note: Total recipe: 20 carbohydrates, 2 fiber, 99 protein.

FUNNEL CAKES

2 eggs
3 T. water
2 T. heavy cream
1 T. oil
1 c. vanilla whey protein
1 T. baking powder
1 tsp. cinnamon
⅓ c. Splenda

Preheat oil to 375°. Combine water, eggs, cream and oil; mix. Then mix in vanilla whey protein, baking powder, cinnamon and Splenda. Pour mixture through a funnel going back and forth, into hot oil. If too thick to go through funnel, add more water. Don't overload fryer so it has room to float. Cook to golden brown, turning over once. Drain on paper towel. If you wish, you can sprinkle with Splenda.

Note: Total recipe: 21 carbohydrates, 2 fiber, 93 protein.

7-UP FUNNEL CAKES

2 eggs
¼ c. Diet 7-Up
1 T. oil
1 c. vanilla whey protein
1 tsp. baking soda
¼ tsp. nutmeg
⅓ c. Splenda

Preheat oil to 375°. Combine eggs, 7-Up and oil; mix. Then mix in vanilla whey protein, baking soda, nutmeg and Splenda. Pour mixture through a funnel going back and forth into hot oil. If too thick to go through funnel, add more water. Don't overload fryer so it has room to float. Cook to golden brown, burning over once. Drain on paper towel. If you wish you can sprinkle with Splenda.

Note: Total recipe: 20 carbohydrates, 2 fiber, 93 protein.

38656-01

Breakfast

Pancakes, Waffles, Eggs, Custard, French Toast, Cereal, Eggs, Mush, Toppings and Fillings

My Favorite Recipe

CINNAMON PANCAKES

1 lg. egg
1 T. oil
½ c. water
2 T. heavy cream
1 T. Vital wheat gluten flour
¾ c. vanilla whey protein
1 tsp. baking powder
½ tsp. cinnamon

Combine the egg, oil, water and heavy cream; mix well. Add gluten flour, whey protein, baking powder and cinnamon. Beat until smooth. Add some oil to your griddle or frying pan and preheat on low, while you are making the pancakes. Pour the batter into the frying pan and turn as soon as they are puffed and full of bubbles.

Note: Total recipe: 11 carbohydrates, 2 fiber and 53 protein.

CHEESE LATKES

Barbara Pollack
Expert Foods

7½ oz. ricotta cheese
2 eggs
¼ c. almond powder
1 T. butter
1 pkg. Sweet One*
1 tsp. vanilla
1 pinch salt
2 T. butter or oil for frying

Almond powder if finely-ground blanched almonds. Blend all ingredients until very smooth. If not using a blender, melt butter first. (*I would use 1 package Splenda - Diana Lee.) Preheat oven pan (50 percent on a 2600-watt burner). Grease generously with butter or oil. Drop batter by spoonfuls into pan. They will form very thin pancakes, much like crepes or blini. Cook (at 40 percent) on first side until bubbly and brown around edges. Be sure to give them enough time to firm up before turning.

Note: Serving based on main dish portion. Size of crepes depends on whether they are being rolled around fillings (1 to 2 tablespoons of batter) or being served like pancakes (½ to 1 tablespoon). Total recipe: 17 carbohydrates, 2 fiber and 44 protein.

COTTAGE CHEESE PANCAKES

Baking Low Carb Bread & Breakfast

2 eggs
¼ c. cottage cheese
2 tsp. Splenda
3 T. natural whey protein
1 T. Vital wheat gluten flour
1 tsp. baking powder

Beat the eggs and add cottage cheese; mix well. Combine Splenda, whey protein, wheat gluten flour and baking powder. Add to cottage cheese mix and beat. Add some oil to your griddle or frying pan and preheat on low, while you are making the pancakes. Keep batter stirred between cakes so the cottage cheese doesn't sink to the bottom. Pour the batter into the frying pan and turn as soon as they are puffed and full of bubbles. Turn and brown on the other side.

Note: Total recipe: 8 carbohydrates, 0 fiber, 35 protein.

30656-01

JEFF'S KILLER LOW CARB PANCAKES

Jeffrey L. David

- 1 c. whole milk ricotta cheese (I use Sorrento brand)
- ½ c. soya powder (I use Fearn brand)*
- ¼ c. wheat bran (I use Arrowhead Mills brand)
- ½ tsp. salt
- ½ tsp. cinnamon
- ⅛ tsp. baking powder (opt.) helps texture a bit
- ¼ c. heavy cream
- 4 lg. eggs
- 1 T. oil (canola or any neutral tasting oil is fine)
- 2 pkgs. artificial sweetener OR ¼ tsp. Stevia liquid*

Combine all dry ingredients in a mixing bowl and stir. Add ricotta and liquid ingredients. With an electric mixer, mix on lowest speed for about 10 seconds, then at highest speed for about another minute. If the batter is too thick, add a tablespoon or two of water or cream. Heat a nonstick griddle (or coat a griddle with vegetable spray). Pour batter onto hot griddle to about 3 to 3.5-inch circles. Cook until bubbles surface on uncooked side, flip and cook until done (about another minute). Serve hot with melted butter or DaVinci Sugar-Free Pancake Syrup. Makes 3 to 4 servings. Will keep well in refrigerator for a couple of days. Cooked pancakes will reheat well in the microwave. Recipe can also be cut in half (½ of ¼ cup is 2 tablespoons.) The size of the eggs and the moisture content of the ricotta cheese will affect the thickness of the batter. A dry ricotta will require adding more cream or some water to the a batter. I have also used 2 whole eggs and 4 egg whites instead of 4 whole eggs. This actually improves the final result somewhat. Some people have told me that this recipe works well substituting soy protein isolate for the soy powder. Doing so will reduce the total carb count to approximately 18 grams. It will also cut the fiber contents in half. Entire recipe carbohydrates, approximately 32 grams and 8 to grams per serving. Also container 3 to 4 grams of fiber per serving. Assumes 2 grams of carbo per ¼ cup of cheese. Check the label, it varies between brans. *I substitute whey protein powder and Sweet 'N Low liquid.

OAT CAKES

- 2 lg. eggs
- 1 tsp. oil
- ⅓ c. water
- 2 T. heavy cream
- ½ c. oat flour
- ¼ c. vanilla whey protein
- ½ tsp. baking powder

Combine the egg, oil, water and heavy cream; mix well. Add oat flour, whey protein and baking powder. Beat until smooth. Add some oil to your griddle or frying pan and preheat on blow, while you are making the pancakes. Pour the batter into the frying pan and turn as soon as they are puffed and full of bubble.

Note: Total recipe: 32 carbohydrates, 4 fiber and 33 protein.

PECAN CAKES

1 lg. eggs
1 tsp. oil
½ c. water
2 T. heavy cream
¼ c. ground pecans
1 c. vanilla whey protein
½ tsp. baking powder

Combine the egg, oil, water and heavy cream; mix well. Add ground pecans, whey protein and baking powder. Beat until smooth. Add some oil to your griddle or frying pan preheat on low, while you are making the pancakes. Pour the batter into the frying pan and turn as soon as they are puffed and full of bubbles.

Note: Total recipe: 16 carbohydrates, 4 fiber and 64 protein.

SWEDISH PANCAKES

3 lg. eggs
1 tsp. oil
½ c. water
½ c. heavy cream
1 T. Vital wheat gluten florr
¾ c. natural whey protein powder
Dash of salt
1 T. Splenda

Combine the egg, oil, water and heavy cream; mix well. Add gluten flour, whey protein, salt and Splenda. Beat until smooth. Add some oil to your griddle or frying pan and preheat on low, while you are making the pancakes. These are thin pancakes. Pour the batter into the frying pan to coat the bottom. Tilt skillet to cover evenly. Lift edges of pancake to see if browning and turn when its a lightly brown.

Note: Total recipe: 15 carbohydrates, 2 fiber and 67 protein.

VANILLA WHEY CAKES

1 lg. egg
1 tsp. oil
2 T. heavy cream
¾ c. vanilla whey protein
¼ tsp. baking powder

Combine the egg, oil and heavy cream; mix well. Add whey protein and baking powder. Beat until smooth. Add some oil to your griddle or frying pan and preheat on low, while you are making the pancakes. Pour the batter into the frying pan and turn as soon as they are puffed and full of bubbles.

Note: Total recipe: 9 carbohydrates, 2 fiber and 47 protein.

38656-01

JEFF'S NEW YEARS WAFFLES

2 lg. eggs, separated
½ c. ricotta cheese
¼ c. soy powder*
2 T. wheat bran
2 T. heavy cream
1 T. cooking oil
¼ tsp. salt
¼ tsp. cinnamon
⅛ tsp. cream of tartar
1 pkt. artificial sweetener OR ⅛ tsp. Stevia liquid*

Place egg whites in a bowl with the cream of tartar and beat until stiff but not dry. In a separate bowl, combine remaining ingredients and beat with an electric mixer until smooth. Fold egg whites into mixture until completely blended. Heat waffle iron and pour entire batter onto iron. Cook about 5 minutes or according to manufacturers instructions. Makes 4 (4-inch) waffles. Top with butter, sour cream or a no-cal syrup.

Note: Entire recipe: carbohydrates, approximately 16 grams and 4 grams per waffle. Also, each waffles has approximately 1.5 grams of fiber. *I substitute whey protein powder and Sweet 'N Low liquid.

WAFFLES

3 eggs
½ c. cottage cheese
1 T. oil
2 tsp. Splenda
¼ c. natural whey protein
2 T. Vital wheat gluten flour
2 tsp. baking powder

Beat the eggs and add oil and cottage cheese; mix well. Combine Splenda, whey protein, wheat gluten flour and baking powder. Add to cottage cheese mix and beat. Spray Pam, on your preheated waffle iron. Keep batter stirred between waffles so the cottage cheese doesn't sink to the bottom. Pour the batter into the waffle iron and follow manufactures directions.

Note: Total recipe: 11 carbohydrates, 1 fiber and 50 protein.

38656-01

EGG NESTS

2 eggs
1/4 tsp. cream of tartar
1/8 tsp. salt
1 T. melted butter

Melt butter and set aside. Preheat oven to 350°. Separate eggs carefully into two bowls. You want the yolks to stay whole. Beat egg whites, salt and cream of tartar until real stiff. On a Pam sprayed cookie sheet from two nests from the egg whites. Gently put one egg yolk in the center of each nest. Spoon melted butter over each egg. Bake 10 to 15 minutes depending on how hard you want your yolk.

Note: Total Recipe: 2 carbohydrates, 0 fiber and 12 protein.

EGG, VEGETABLE AND CHEESE CASSEROLE

1/2 c. butter
14 eggs
1/2 c. water
1/4 tsp. garlic salt
3/4 c. heavy whipping cream
2 c. cooked ham or sausage
1/2 c. green pepper
1/2 c. chopped onions
1 c. sliced mushrooms
1 c. shredded cheddar cheese

Melt butter in a frying pan and sauté ham or sausage, pepper, onions and mushrooms until vegetables are tender. When done pour into a 9 x 13-inch baking pan. Beat eggs, water and whipping cream until combined. Spoon over the top of the meat and vegetables. Sprinkle with cheese on top. Bake at 350° for 20 minutes covered and then 20 minutes, uncovered. Let set 5 to 10 minutes before serving.

Note: Total recipe: 32 carbohydrates, 3 fiber and 167 protein.

CHEESE OVEN OMELET

10 eggs
1/2 c. water
1/2 c. heavy whipping cream
1 1/2 c. shredded Cheddar cheese
1/2 tsp. onion salt

Combine eggs, water and whipping cream and beat. Stir in cheese and onion salt. Pour into Pam sprayed 8-inch baking dish. Bake at 325° for 40 to 45 minutes or until omelet is set and top golden brown.

Note: Total recipe: 12 carbohydrates, 0 fiber and 96 protein.

38656-01

MEXICAN OVEN OMELET

8 eggs
¼ c. water
¼ c. heavy whipping cream
1 c. shredded cheddar cheese
¼ c. canned, chopped green chilies
¼ c. sliced, ripe olives
⅛ tsp. onion salt
2 T. melted butter
3 T. sour cream
3 T. taco sauce

Combine eggs, water and whipping cream and beat. Stir in cheese, chilies, olives and onion salt. Pour into a Pam sprayed 8-inch baking dish. Bake at 325° for 40 to 45 minutes or until omelet is set and top golden brown. Top with sour cream and taco sauce.

Note: Total recipe: 189 carbohydrates, 1 fiber and 74 protein.

CHEESE QUICHE

4 eggs
½ c. heavy whipping cream
½ tsp. dry mustard
⅛ tsp. garlic salt
½ c. grated cheese, Swiss or Cheddar
½ c. bacon bits

Combine eggs, whipping cream, mustard and garlic salt; beat. Stir in cheese and bacon. Pour into a Pam sprayed 8-inch baking dish. Bake at 350° for 35 to 40 minutes or until quiche is set and top golden brown.

Note: Total recipe: 7 carbohydrates, 0 fiber and 50 protein.

SPINACH QUICHE

6 eggs
¼ c. water
4 oz. cream cheese, room temperature
1¼ c. cheddar cheese
½ tsp. salt
1 pkg. frozen, chopped spinach, thawed & drained

Combine eggs, water, cream cheese and beat. Stir in cheese, salt and spinach. Pour into a Pam sprayed 8-inch baking dish. Bake at 325° for 40 to 45 minutes or until omelet is set and top golden brown.

Note: Total recipe 21 carbohydrates, 9 fiber and 81 protein.

BREAKFAST CUSTARD

4 lg. eggs
4 oz. Mascarpone cheese
¼ c. heavy whipping cream
¼ c. Splenda
½ tsp. cinnamon
⅛ tsp. nutmeg
1 T. melted butter

Mix eggs, cheese, heavy whipping cream, Splenda, cinnamon, nutmeg and melted butter. Pour into a small baking dish coated with Pam. Bake at 350° for 20 to 30 minutes until knife inserted in middle comes out clean.

Note: Total recipe: 17 carbohydrates, 1 fiber and 33 protein.

FRENCH TOAST

3 eggs
⅓ c. water
⅓ c. heavy whipping cream
1 T. Splenda
¼ tsp. vanilla
¼ tsp. cinnamon
8 slices of your favorite low carbohydrate bread, sliced ½ inch thick

Beat eggs, water, whipping cream, Splenda, vanilla and cinnamon until well blended. Dip bread into egg mixture and coat each side. Place in preheated frying pan with hot oil. Cook on both sides until brown.

Note: 5 carbohydrates, 0 fiber and 18 protein. These counts are without the bread. Add to these counts according to bread you use.

OVEN FRENCH TOAST

3 eggs
⅓ c. water
⅓ c. heavy whipping cream
1 T. Splenda
¼ tsp. vanilla
¼ tsp. cinnamon
8 slices of your favorite low carb bread, sliced ½ inch thick

Beat eggs, water, whipping cream, Splenda, vanilla and cinnamon until well blended. Dip bread into egg mixture and coat each side. Preheat a generously oiled jelly-roll pan (15½ x 10½ x 1 inch). Preheat about 1 minute. After baking form oven, place your dipped bread sliced on the pan. Bake at 350° for about 5 to 8 minutes until bottoms are light brown. Turn bread and cook another 2 to 5 minutes longer.

Note: 5 carbohydrates, 0 fiber and 18 proteins. These counts are without the bread. Add to these counts according to bread you use.

38656-01

Breakfast

ALMOST OATMEAL

3 T. "Designer Protein" natural whey protein powder
2 T. quick oatmeal (cook in 1 minute)
1½ tsp. Expert Foods thicken thin not/sugar
⅛ tsp. salt
⅛ tsp. molasses
¼ c. water

Whisk whey protein, oatmeal and thicken thin together. Add salt, molasses, water and mix until combined. Microwave for 30 seconds. Stir. Microwave again. If you want it thicker, continue to microwave. Serve with cream.

Note: Total recipe 9 carbohydrates, 3 fiber and 20 protein.

BRAN CEREAL

¼ c. Ketschmer toasted wheat bran
1 scoop "Designer Protein" French vanilla whey protein powder
¼ tsp. cinnamon
1 tsp. Splenda
⅓ c. water

Whisk bran, whey protein, cinnamon and Splenda together. Add water and mix until combined. Microwave for 30 seconds. Stir. Microwave again. If you want it thicker, continue to microwave. Serve with cream.

Note: Total recipe: 13 carbohydrates, 7 fiber and 20 protein.

HOT CHOCOLATE BRAN CEREAL

¼ c. Kretschmer toasted wheat bran
1 pkg. Swiss Miss Diet hot chocolate
1 scoop "Designer Protein" French vanilla whey protein powder
1 T. ground almonds
⅓ c. water

Whisk bran, hot chocolate mix, whey protein and almonds together. Add water and mix until combined. Microwave for 30 seconds. Stir, Microwave again. If you want it thicker, continue to microwave. Serve with cream.

Note: Total recipe: 17 carbohydrates, 9 fiber and 20 protein.

HOT CEREAL

1 scoop "Designer Protein" natural whey protein powder
2 T. ground almonds or ground flax seed
2 T. melted butter
1/8 tsp. salt
1/4 c. water

Whisk whey protein and almonds together. Add water and mix until combined. Microwave for 30 seconds. Stir. Microwave again. If you want it thicker, continue to microwave. Serve with cream.

Note: Total recipe: 5 carbohydrates, 2 fiber and 20 protein.

FRIED MUSH

4 lg. egg
1/2 c. ricotta cheese
1/4 c. heavy whipping cream
2 T. Splenda
1/2 tsp. cinnamon
1 tsp. oil

Mix eggs, cheese, heavy whipping cream, Splenda, cinnamon, nutmeg and oil. Pour into a 8 x 8 -inch baking dish coated with Pam. Bake at 350° for 20 to 30 minutes until knife inserted in middle comes out clean. Cut into fourths and fry in hot oil in frying pan until brown on both sides. Serve with your favorite topping.

Note: Total recipe 12 carbohydrates, 1 fiber and 40 protein.

MAPLE BUTTER

1 stick softened butter
2 T. Splenda
1 tsp. maple extract

Whip butter, Splenda and maple extract. Serve on pancakes or waffles instead of syrup.

Note: Total recipe 3 carbohydrates, 0 fiber and 0 protein.

NUT BUTTER SPREAD

1 c. walnuts or almonds
1 stick butter
1/4 c. Splenda

Cream butter and Splenda until fluffy. Put walnuts in blender and use high speed until walnuts are powdered. Add walnuts to butter mixture and mix until smooth.

Note: Approximately 28 carbohydrates, 15 fiber and 17 protein.

38656-01

LOWCARB BLACKBERRY FRUIT SPREAD

Barbara Pollack

½ pt. blackberries (5 oz.)
⅓ c. water
1 tsp. lemon juice
Pinch salt (opt.)
4 T. Splenda
3½ T. Thick Thin not/sugar

Put berries with water to just barely cover. (The amount in the recipe is just an estimate) in saucepan, cover and simmer until softened and juicy. Mash to desired texture. Use well-mashed fruit for jam-like spread, but leave recognizable pieces if you want it to resemble preserves. Add lemon juice, salt and sweetener to taste. Again, the amounts in our recipe are just estimates; please adjust the amounts to flavor it to your taste. Add not/sugar to thicken to slightly less than desired thickness as it will continue to thicken somewhat as it cools. Refrigerate.

Note about cooking time: While you need to cook the fruit only enough to soften it, your fruit spread will keep longer if the fruit is cooked thoroughly. Per tablespoons 2.5 carbohydrates, 1.4 fiber and 1 protein.

PUDDING FILLING

1 pkg. sugar free pudding
¾ c. heavy whipping cream
1 c. water

Follow direction on pudding package.

Note: Total recipe: 29 carbohydrates, 0 fiber and 4 protein.

CREAM CHEESE FROSTING

4 oz. cream cheese (room temperature)
2 T. butter, softened
½ c. Splenda
½ tsp. heavy whipping cream
1 tsp. almond extract

Mix Splenda, extract and whipping cream together until Splenda dissolves. Beat with butter and cream cheese until fluffy.

Note: Total recipe: 16 carbohydrates, 0 fiber and 6 protein.

GLAZE

4 T. unsalted butter
2 T. Splenda
½ tsp. extract
1 T. cream

Melt butter and stir in Splenda. Add your favorite extract and cream. For different flavors you might want to add ⅛ teaspoon orange Kool-Aid mix or substitute 1 tablespoon of Splenda with Spoonable brown sugar by Sugar Twin.

Note: Total recipe: 3.5 carbohydrate, 0 fiber and 0 protein.

Recipe Favorites

38656-01

INDEX OF RECIPES

YEAST BREAD & ROLLS

APPLE CIDER ROLLS 23
BISMARCKS 24
BRAN BREAD 1
CHOCOLATE FILLED DANISH ROLLS 25
CINNAMON BREAD 2
CINNAMON ROLLS 26
CREAM CHEESE DANISH ROLLS 27
DILL ONION BREAD 3
DINNER ROLLS 19
FLAX BREAD 4
GARLIC BREAD 5
GINGERBREAD 6
ITALIAN HERB BREAD 7
MACADAMIA COCONUT HORSESHOE 29
OAT NUT BREAD 8
ONION AND CHEESE BREAD 9
ORANGE NUT HORSESHOE 30
PARMESAN GARLIC BREAD 10
PEACHY CREAM CINNAMON ROLLS 28
PECAN HORSESHOE 31
PUMPERNICKEL 11
RANCH BREAD 12
RHUBARB KUCHEN 22
RYE BREAD 13
RYE DINNER ROLLS 20
SOUR CREAM KUCHEN 21
SPICY SWEET BREAD 14
SQUARE HAMBURGER BUNS 18
TOMATO ROSEMARY BREAD 15
WHEAT BREAD 16
WHITE BREAD 17

QUICK BREADS

APPLE BRAN MUFFINS 35
APPLE FRITTERS 58
APPLE FUNNEL CAKES 59
BANANA CHOCOLATE CHIP MUFFINS 36
BANANA ORANGE LOAF 45
BANANA PEANUT BUTTER MUFFINS 36
BANANA WALNUT MUFFINS 37
BISCUITS 33
BLUEBERRY COFFEE CAKE 43
BLUEBERRY MUFFINS 38
BRAN MUFFINS 37
CARAWAY RYE CRACKERS 49
CARROT LOAF 46
CARROT MUFFINS 38
CARROT ZUCCHINI LOAF 46
CHEESE BISCUITS 33
CHEESE CRACKERS 50
CHOCOLATE COFFEE CAKE 44
CHOCOLATE RIPPLE COFFEE CAKE 44
CHOCOLATE WHISKEY MUFFINS 39
CHOCOLATE ZUCCHINI LOAF 47
CINNAMON FRITTERS 59
COCOA DONUT PUFFS 57
CORN CRACKERS 51
COTTAGE CHEESE BISCUITS 34
CRANBERRY LOAF 47
DONUT PUFFS 58
FLAX MUFFINS 39
FUNNEL CAKES 60
HEALTHY MUFFINS 40
MOCHA MUFFINS 40
ONION CRACKERS 53
ONION FRITTERS 59
ORANGE CARROT MUFFINS 41
PEANUT BUTTER COFFEE CAKE 45
PIZZA DOUGH 57
POPOVERS 56
POPPY SEED CRACKERS 54
POPPY SEED MUFFINS 41
RASPBERRY MUFFINS 42
RHUBARB MUFFINS 42
RYE-FLAVORED SEED FLATBREAD/CRACKERS 52
SCONES 56
7-UP FUNNEL CAKES 60
SOUR CREAM BISCUITS 34
STRAWBERRY RHUBARB LOAF 48
SUNFLOWER PARMESAN CRACKERS 55
SWEET BRAN LOAF 48
SWEET CRACKERS 55
SWEET DROP BISCUITS/ SHORTCAKE 35
SWEET POTATO LOAF 49
SWEET POTATO MUFFINS 43

BREAKFAST

ALMOST OATMEAL 69
BRAN CEREAL 69
BREAKFAST CUSTARD 68
CHEESE LATKES 61
CHEESE OVEN OMELET 66
CHEESE QUICHE 67
CINNAMON PANCAKES 61
COTTAGE CHEESE PANCAKES 62
CREAM CHEESE FROSTING 71

EGG NESTS 66
EGG, VEGETABLE AND CHEESE CASSEROLE 66
FRENCH TOAST 68
FRIED MUSH 70
GLAZE 72
HOT CEREAL 70
HOT CHOCOLATE BRAN CEREAL 69
JEFF'S KILLER LOW CARB PANCAKES 63
JEFF'S NEW YEARS WAFFLES 65
LOWCARB BLACKBERRY FRUIT SPREAD 71
MAPLE BUTTER 70
MEXICAN OVEN OMELET 67
NUT BUTTER SPREAD 70
OAT CAKES 63
OVEN FRENCH TOAST 68
PECAN CAKES 64
PUDDING FILLING 71
SPINACH QUICHE 67
SWEDISH PANCAKES 64
VANILLA WHEY CAKES 64
WAFFLES 65

How to Order

Get your additional copies of this cookbook by returning an order form and your check or money order to:

Diana Lee
315 W. Northwest Hwy
Palatine, IL 60010

Current pricing can be found at:
http://pages.prodigy.net/dls1015/

✂- -

Please send me _____ copies of the **Baking Low Carb Bread & Breakfast** cookbook at **$**_____ per copy and **$**_____ for shipping and handling per book. Enclosed is my check or money order for $________.

Mail Books To:

Name ____

Address ____

City _______________________ State ____ Zip _______

✂- -

Please send me _____ copies of the **Baking Low Carb Bread & Breakfast** cookbook at **$**_____ per copy and **$**_____ for shipping and handling per book. Enclosed is my check or money order for $________.

Mail Books To:

Name ____

Address ____

City _______________________ State ____ Zip _______

38656-jh

Cooking Tips

1. After stewing a chicken, cool in broth before cutting into chunks; it will have twice the flavor.

2. To slice meat into thin strips, as for stir-fry dishes, partially freeze it so it will slice more easily.

3. A roast with the bone in will cook faster than a boneless roast. The bone carries the heat to the inside more quickly.

4. When making a roast, place dry onion soup mix in the bottom of your roaster pan. After removing the roast, add 1 can of mushroom soup and you will have a good brown gravy.

5. For a juicier hamburger, add cold water to the beef before grilling (1/2 cup to 1 pound of meat).

6. To freeze meatballs, place them on a cookie sheet until frozen. Place in plastic bags. They will stay separated so that you may remove as many as you want.

7. To keep cauliflower white while cooking, add a little milk to the water.

8. When boiling corn, add sugar to the water instead of salt. Salt will toughen the corn.

9. To ripen tomatoes, put them in a brown paper bag in a dark pantry, and they will ripen overnight.

10. To keep celery crisp, stand it upright in a pitcher of cold, salted water and refrigerate.

11. When cooking cabbage, place a small tin cup or can half full of vinegar on the stove near the cabbage. It will absorb the odor.

12. Potatoes soaked in salt water for 20 minutes before baking will bake more rapidly.

13. Let raw potatoes stand in cold water for at least a half-hour before frying in order to improve the crispness of French-fried potatoes. Dry potatoes thoroughly before adding to oil.

14. Use greased muffin tins as molds when baking stuffed green peppers.

15. A few drops of lemon juice in the water will whiten boiled potatoes.

16. Buy mushrooms before they "open." When stems and caps are attached firmly, mushrooms are truly fresh.

17. Do not use metal bowls when mixing salads. Use wood, glass or china.

18. Lettuce keeps better if you store it in the refrigerator without washing it. Keep the leaves dry. Wash lettuce the day you are going to use it.

19. Do not use soda to keep vegetables green. It destroys Vitamin C.

20. Do not despair if you oversalt gravy. Stir in some instant mashed potatoes to repair the damage. Just add a little more liquid in order to offset the thickening.

Herbs & Spices

Acquaint yourself with herbs and spices. Add in small amounts, 1/4 teaspoon for every 4 servings. Crush dried herbs or snip fresh ones before using. Use 3 times more fresh herbs if substituting fresh for dried.

Basil	Sweet, warm flavor with an aromatic odor. Use whole or ground. Good with lamb, fish, roast, stews, ground beef, vegetables, dressing and omelets.
Bay Leaves	Pungent flavor. Use whole leaf but remove before serving. Good in vegetable dishes, seafood, stews and pickles.
Caraway	Spicy taste and aromatic smell. Use in cakes, breads, soups, cheese and sauerkraut.
Chives	Sweet, mild flavor like that of onion. Excellent in salads, fish, soups and potatoes.
Cilantro	Use fresh. Excellent in salads, fish, chicken, rice, beans and Mexican dishes.
Curry Powder	Spices are combined to proper proportions to give a distinct flavor to meat, poultry, fish and vegetables.
Dill	Both seeds and leaves are flavorful. Leaves may be used as a garnish or cooked with fish, soup, dressings, potatoes and beans. Leaves or the whole plant may be used to flavor pickles.
Fennel	Sweet, hot flavor. Both seeds and leaves are used. Use in small quantities in pies and baked goods. Leaves can be boiled with fish.
Ginger	A pungent root, this aromatic spice is sold fresh, dried or ground. Use in pickles, preserves, cakes, cookies, soups and meat dishes.

Herbs & Spices

Marjoram	May be used both dried or green. Use to flavor fish, poultry, omelets, lamb, stew, stuffing and tomato juice.
Mint	Aromatic with a cool flavor. Excellent in beverages, fish, lamb, cheese, soup, peas, carrots, and fruit desserts.
Oregano	Strong, aromatic odor. Use whole or ground in tomato juice, fish, eggs, pizza, omelets, chili, stew, gravy, poultry and vegetables.
Paprika	A bright red pepper, this spice is used in meat, vegetables and soups or as a garnish for potatoes, salads or eggs.
Parsley	Best when used fresh, but can be used dried as a garnish or as a seasoning. Try in fish, omelets, soup, meat, stuffing and mixed greens.
Rosemary	Very aromatic. Can be used fresh or dried. Season fish, stuffing, beef, lamb, poultry, onions, eggs, bread and potatoes. Great in dressings.
Saffron	Orange-yellow in color, this spice flavors or colors foods. Use in soup, chicken, rice and breads.
Sage	Use fresh or dried. The flowers are sometimes used in salads. May be used in tomato juice, fish, omelets, beef, poultry, stuffing, cheese spreads and breads.
Tarragon	Leaves have a pungent, hot taste. Use to flavor sauces, salads, fish, poultry, tomatoes, eggs, green beans, carrots and dressings.
Thyme	Sprinkle leaves on fish or poultry before broiling or baking. Throw a few sprigs directly on coals shortly before meat is finished grilling.

Baking Breads

Hints for Baking Breads

1. Kneading dough for 30 seconds after mixing improves the texture of baking powder biscuits.

2. Instead of shortening, use cooking or salad oil in waffles and hot cakes.

3. When bread is baking, a small dish of water in the oven will help keep the crust from hardening.

4. Dip a spoon in hot water to measure shortening, butter, etc., and the fat will slip out more easily.

5. Small amounts of leftover corn may be added to pancake batter for variety.

6. To make bread crumbs, use the fine cutter of a food grinder and tie a large paper bag over the spout in order to prevent flying crumbs.

7. When you are doing any sort of baking, you get better results if you remember to preheat your cookie sheet, muffin tins or cake pans.

Rules for Use of Leavening Agents

1. In simple flour mixtures, use 2 teaspoons baking powder to leaven 1 cup flour. Reduce this amount 1/2 teaspoon for each egg used.

2. To 1 teaspoon soda use 2 1/4 teaspoons cream of tartar, 2 cups freshly soured milk, or 1 cup molasses.

3. To substitute soda and an acid for baking powder, divide the amount of baking powder by 4. Take that as your measure and add acid according to rule 2.

Proportions of Baking Powder to Flour

biscuits ....to 1 cup flour use 1 1/4 tsp. baking powder
cake with oil ....to 1 cup flour use 1 tsp. baking powder
muffins ....to 1 cup flour use 1 1/2 tsp. baking powder
popovers ....to 1 cup flour use 1 1/4 tsp. baking powder
waffles ....to 1 cup flour use 1 1/4 tsp. baking powder

Proportions of Liquid to Flour

drop batter ....to 1 cup liquid use 2 to 2 1/2 cups flour
pour batter ....to 1 cup liquid use 1 cup flour
soft dough ....to 1 cup liquid use 3 to 3 1/2 cups flour
stiff dough ....to 1 cup liquid use 4 cups flour

Time and Temperature Chart

Breads	Minutes	Temperature
biscuits	12 - 15	400° - 450°
cornbread	25 - 30	400° - 425°
gingerbread	40 - 50	350° - 370°
loaf	50 - 60	350° - 400°
nut bread	50 - 75	350°
popovers	30 - 40	425° - 450°
rolls	20 - 30	400° - 450°

Baking Desserts

Perfect Cookies

Cookie dough that is to be rolled is much easier to handle after it has been refrigerated for 10 to 30 minutes. This keeps the dough from sticking, even though it may be soft. If not done, the soft dough may require more flour and too much flour makes cookies hard and brittle. Place on a floured board only as much dough as can be easily managed. Flour the rolling pin slightly and roll lightly to desired thickness. Cut shapes close together and add trimmings to dough that needs to be rolled. Place pans or sheets in upper third of oven. Watch cookies carefully while baking in order to avoid burned edges. When sprinkling sugar on cookies, try putting it into a salt shaker in order to save time.

Perfect Pies

1. Pie crust will be better and easier to make if all the ingredients are cool.
2. The lower crust should be placed in the pan so that it covers the surface smoothly. Air pockets beneath the surface will push the crust out of shape while baking.
3. Folding the top crust over the lower crust before crimping will keep juices in the pie.
4. In making custard pie, bake at a high temperature for about ten minutes to prevent a soggy crust. Then finish baking at a low temperature.
5. When making cream pie, sprinkle crust with powdered sugar in order to prevent it from becoming soggy.

Perfect Cakes

1. Fill cake pans two-thirds full and spread batter into corners and sides, leaving a slight hollow in the center.
2. Cake is done when it shrinks from the sides of the pan or if it springs back when touched lightly with the finger.
3. After removing a cake from the oven, place it on a rack for about five minutes. Then, the sides should be loosened and the cake turned out on a rack in order to finish cooling.
4. Do not frost cakes until thoroughly cool.
5. Icing will remain where you put it if you sprinkle cake with powdered sugar first.

Time and Temperature Chart

Dessert	Time	Temperature
butter cake, layer	20-40 min.	380° - 400°
butter cake, loaf	40-60 min.	360° - 400°
cake, angel	50-60 min.	300° - 360°
cake, fruit	3-4 hrs.	275° - 325°
cake, sponge	40-60 min.	300° - 350°
cookies, molasses	18-20 min.	350° - 375°
cookies, thin	10-12 min.	380° - 390°
cream puffs	45-60 min.	300° - 350°
meringue	40-60 min.	250° - 300°
pie crust	20-40 min.	400° - 500°

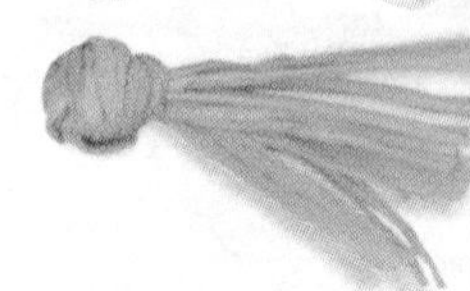

Vegetables & Fruits

Vegetable	Cooking Method	Time
artichokes	boiled	40 min.
	steamed	45-60 min.
asparagus tips	boiled	10-15 min.
beans, lima	boiled	20-40 min.
	steamed	60 min.
beans, string	boiled	15-35 min.
	steamed	60 min.
beets, old	boiled or steamed	1-2 hours
beets, young with skin	boiled	30 min.
	steamed	60 min.
	baked	70-90 min.
broccoli, flowerets	boiled	5-10 min.
broccoli, stems	boiled	20-30 min.
brussels sprouts	boiled	20-30 min.
cabbage, chopped	boiled	10-20 min.
	steamed	25 min.
carrots, cut across	boiled	8-10 min.
	steamed	40 min.
cauliflower, flowerets	boiled	8-10 min.
cauliflower, stem down	boiled	20-30 min.
corn, green, tender	boiled	5-10 min.
	steamed	15 min.
	baked	20 min.
corn on the cob	boiled	8-10 min.
	steamed	15 min.
eggplant, whole	boiled	30 min.
	steamed	40 min.
	baked	45 min.
parsnips	boiled	25-40 min.
	steamed	60 min.
	baked	60-75 min.
peas, green	boiled or steamed	5-15 min.
potatoes	boiled	20-40 min.
	steamed	60 min.
	baked	45-60 min.
pumpkin or squash	boiled	20-40 min.
	steamed	45 min.
	baked	60 min.
tomatoes	boiled	5-15 min.
turnips	boiled	25-40 min.

Drying Time Table

Fruit	Sugar or Honey	Cooking Time
apricots	1/4 c. for each cup of fruit	about 40 min.
figs	1 T. for each cup of fruit	about 30 min.
peaches	1/4 c. for each cup of fruit	about 45 min.
prunes	2 T. for each cup of fruit	about 45 min.

Vegetables & Fruits

Buying Fresh Vegetables

Artichokes: Look for compact, tightly closed heads with green, clean-looking leaves. Avoid those with leaves that are brown or separated.

Asparagus: Stalks should be tender and firm; tips should be close and compact. Choose the stalks with very little white; they are more tender. Use asparagus soon because it toughens rapidly.

Beans, Snap: Those with small seeds inside the pods are best. Avoid beans with dry-looking pods.

Broccoli, Brussels Sprouts and Cauliflower: Flower clusters on broccoli and cauliflower should be tight and close together. Brussels sprouts should be firm and compact. Smudgy, dirty spots may indicate pests or disease.

Cabbage and Head Lettuce: Choose heads that are heavy for their size. Avoid cabbage with worm holes and lettuce with discoloration or soft rot.

Cucumbers: Choose long, slender cucumbers for best quality. May be dark or medium green, but yellow ones are undesirable.

Mushrooms: Caps should be closed around the stems. Avoid black or brown gills.

Peas and Lima Beans: Select pods that are well-filled but not bulging. Avoid dried, spotted, yellow, or flabby pods.

Buying Fresh Fruits

Bananas: Skin should be free of bruises and black or brown spots. Purchase them green and allow them to ripen at home at room temperature.

Berries: Select plump, solid berries with good color. Avoid stained containers which indicate wet or leaky berries. Berries with clinging caps, such as blackberries and raspberries, may be unripe. Strawberries without caps may be overripe.

Melons: In cantaloupes, thick, close netting on the rind indicates best quality. Cantaloupes are ripe when the stem scar is smooth and the space between the netting is yellow or yellow-green. They are best when fully ripe with fruity odor.

Honeydews are ripe when rind has creamy to yellowish color and velvety texture. Immature honeydews are whitish-green.

Ripe watermelons have some yellow color on one side. If melons are white or pale green on one side, they are not ripe.

Oranges, Grapefruit and Lemons: Choose those heavy for their size. Smoother, thinner skins usually indicate more juice. Most skin markings do not affect quality. Oranges with a slight greenish tinge may be just as ripe as fully colored ones. Light or greenish-yellow lemons are more tart than deep yellow ones. Avoid citrus fruits showing withered, sunken or soft areas.

Napkin Folding

General Tips:

Use well-starched linen napkins if possible. For more complicated folds, 24-inch napkins work best. Practice the folds with newspapers. Children can help. Once they learn the folds, they will have fun!

Shield

Easy fold. Elegant with monogram in corner.

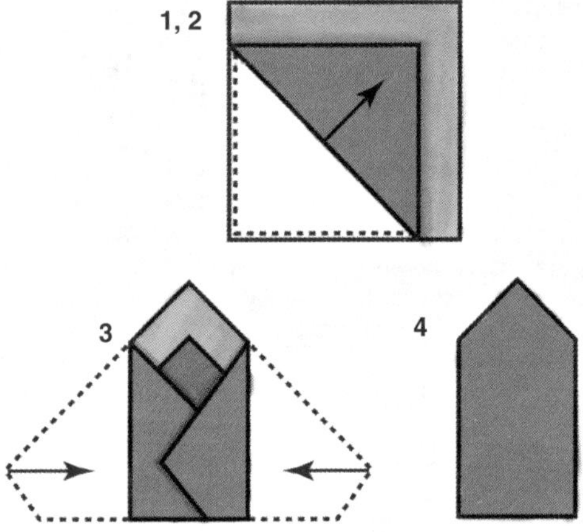

Instructions:

1. Fold into quarter size. If monogrammed, ornate corner should face down.
2. Turn up folded corner three-quarters.
3. Overlap right side and left side points.
4. Turn over; adjust sides so that they are even, single point in center.
5. Place point up or down on plate, or left of plate.

Rosette

Elegant on plate.

Instructions:

1. Fold left and right edges to center, leaving 1/2" opening along center.
2. Pleat firmly from top edge to bottom edge. Sharpen edges with hot iron.
3. Pinch center together. If necessary, use small piece of pipe cleaner to secure and top with single flower.
4. Spread out rosette.

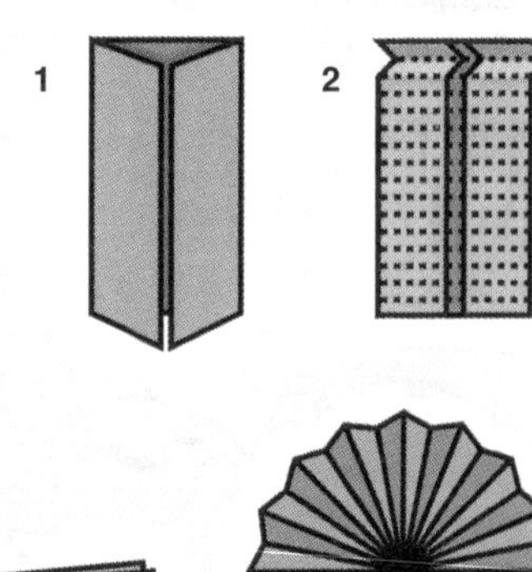

Napkin Folding

Candle

Easy to do; can be decorated.

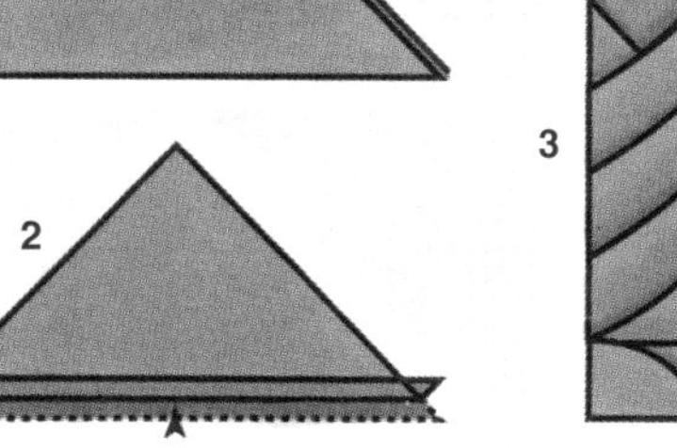

Instructions:
1. Fold into triangle, point at top.
2. Turn lower edge up 1".
3. Turn over, folded edge down.
4. Roll tightly from left to right.
5. Tuck in corner. Stand upright.

Fan

Pretty in napkin ring or on plate.

Instructions:
1. Fold top and bottom edges to center.
2. Fold top and bottom edges to center a second time.
3. Pleat firmly from the left edge. Sharpen edges with hot iron.
4. Spread out fan. Balance flat folds of each side on table. Well-starched napkins will hold shape.

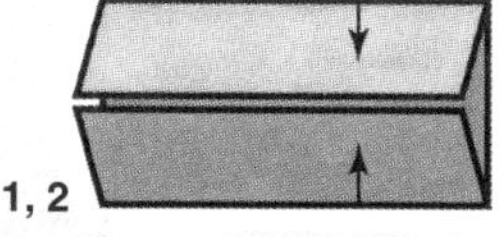

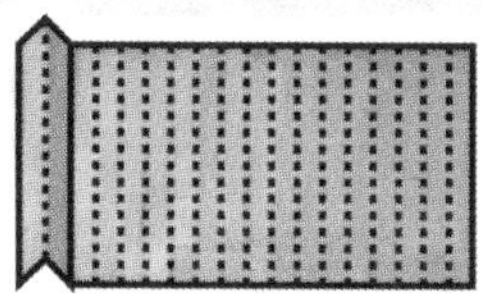

Lily

Effective and pretty on table.

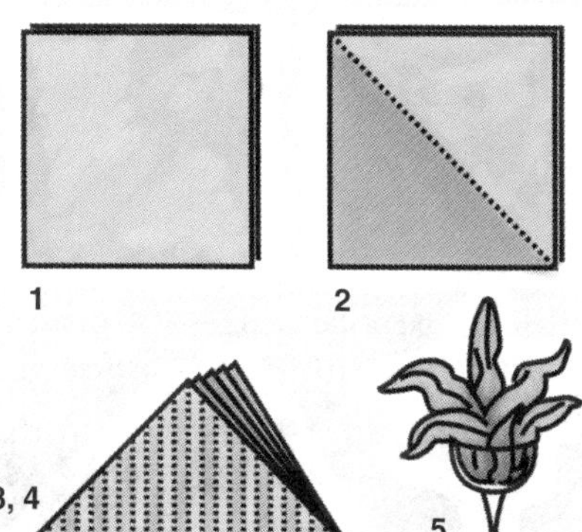

Instructions:
1. Fold napkin into quarters.
2. Fold into triangle, closed corner to open points.
3. Turn two points over to other side. (Two points are on either side of closed point.)
4. Pleat.
5. Place closed end in glass. Pull down two points on each side and shape.

Measurements & Substitutions

Measurements

a pinch	1/8 teaspoon or less
3 teaspoons	1 tablespoon
4 tablespoons	1/4 cup
8 tablespoons	1/2 cup
12 tablespoons	3/4 cup
16 tablespoons	1 cup
2 cups	1 pint
4 cups	1 quart
4 quarts	1 gallon
8 quarts	1 peck
4 pecks	1 bushel
16 ounces	1 pound
32 ounces	1 quart
1 ounce liquid	2 tablespoons
8 ounces liquid	1 cup

Use standard measuring spoons and cups.
All measurements are level.

Substitutions

Ingredient	Quantity	Substitute
baking powder	1 teaspoon	1/4 tsp. baking soda plus 1/2 tsp. cream of tartar
catsup or chili sauce	1 cup	1 c. tomato sauce plus 1/2 c. sugar and 2 T. vinegar (for use in cooking)
chocolate	1 square (1 oz.)	3 or 4 T. cocoa plus 1 T. butter
cornstarch	1 tablespoon	2 T. flour or 2 tsp. quick-cooking tapioca
cracker crumbs	3/4 cup	1 c. bread crumbs
dates	1 lb.	1 1/2 c. dates, pitted and cut
dry mustard	1 teaspoon	1 T. prepared mustard
flour, self-rising	1 cup	1 c. all-purpose flour, 1/2 tsp. salt, and 1 tsp. baking powder
herbs, fresh	1 tablespoon	1 tsp. dried herbs
milk, sour	1 cup	1 T. lemon juice or vinegar plus sweet milk to make 1 c. (let stand 5 minutes)
whole	1 cup	1/2 c. evaporated milk plus 1/2 c. water
min. marshmallows	10	1 lg. marshmallow
onion, fresh	1 small	1 T. instant minced onion, rehydrated
sugar, brown	1/2 cup	2 T. molasses in 1/2 c. granulated sugar
powdered	1 cup	1 c. granulated sugar plus 1 tsp. cornstarch
tomato juice	1 cup	1/2 c. tomato sauce plus 1/2 c. water

When substituting cocoa for chocolate in cakes, the amount of flour must be reduced. Brown and white sugars usually can be interchanged.

Equivalency Chart

Food	Quantity	Yield
apple	1 medium	1 cup
banana, mashed	1 medium	1/3 cup
bread	1 1/2 slices	1 cup soft crumbs
bread	1 slice	1/4 cup fine, dry crumbs
butter	1 stick or 1/4 pound	1/2 cup
cheese, American, cubed	1 pound	2 2/3 cups
American, grated	1 pound	5 cups
cream cheese	3-ounce package	6 2/3 tablespoons
chocolate, bitter	1 square	1 ounce
cocoa	1 pound	4 cups
coconut	1 1/2 pound package	2 2/3 cups
coffee, ground	1 pound	5 cups
cornmeal	1 pound	3 cups
cornstarch	1 pound	3 cups
crackers, graham	14 squares	1 cup fine crumbs
saltine	28 crackers	1 cup fine crumbs
egg	4-5 whole	1 cup
whites	8-10	1 cup
yolks	10-12	1 cup
evaporated milk	1 cup	3 cups whipped
flour, cake, sifted	1 pound	4 1/2 cups
rye	1 pound	5 cups
white, sifted	1 pound	4 cups
white, unsifted	1 pound	3 3/4 cups
gelatin, flavored	3 1/4 ounces	1/2 cup
unflavored	1/4 ounce	1 tablespoon
lemon	1 medium	3 tablespoon juice
marshmallows	16	1/4 pound
noodles, cooked	8-ounce package	7 cups
uncooked	4 ounces (1 1/2 cups)	2-3 cups cooked
macaroni, cooked	8-ounce package	6 cups
macaroni, uncooked	4 ounces (1 1/4 cups)	2 1/4 cups cooked
spaghetti, uncooked	7 ounces	4 cups cooked
nuts, chopped	1/4 pound	1 cup
almonds	1 pound	3 1/2 cups
walnuts, broken	1 pound	3 cups
walnuts, unshelled	1 pound	1 1/2 to 1 3/4 cups
onion	1 medium	1/2 cup
orange	3-4 medium	1 cup juice
raisins	1 pound	3 1/2 cups
rice, brown	1 cup	4 cups cooked
converted	1 cup	3 1/2 cups cooked
regular	1 cup	3 cups cooked
wild	1 cup	4 cups cooked
sugar, brown	1 pound	2 1/2 cups
powdered	1 pound	3 1/2 cups
white	1 pound	2 cups
vanilla wafers	22	1 cup fine crumbs
zwieback, crumbled	4	1 cups

Food Quantities

For Large Servings

	25 Servings	50 Servings	100 Servings
Beverages:			
coffee	1/2 pound and 1 1/2 gallons water	1 pound and 3 gallons water	2 pounds and 6 gallons water
lemonade	10-15 lemons and 1 1/2 gallons water	20-30 lemons and 3 gallons water	40-60 lemons and 6 gallons water
tea	1/12 pound and 1 1/2 gallons water	1/6 pound and 3 gallons water	1/3 pound and 6 gallons water
Desserts:			
layered cake	1 12" cake	3 10" cakes	6 10" cakes
sheet cake	1 10" x 12" cake	1 12" x 20" cake	2 12" x 20" cakes
watermelon	37 1/2 pounds	75 pounds	150 pounds
whipping cream	3/4 pint	1 1/2 to 2 pints	3-4 pints
Ice cream:			
brick	3 1/4 quarts	6 1/2 quarts	13 quarts
bulk	2 1/4 quarts	4 1/2 quarts or 1 1/4 gallons	9 quarts or 2 1/2 gallons
Meat, poultry or fish:			
fish	13 pounds	25 pounds	50 pounds
fish, fillets or steak	7 1/2 pounds	15 pounds	30 pounds
hamburger	9 pounds	18 pounds	35 pounds
turkey or chicken	13 pounds	25 to 35 pounds	50 to 75 pounds
wieners (beef)	6 1/2 pounds	13 pounds	25 pounds
Salads, casseroles:			
baked beans	3/4 gallon	1 1/4 gallons	2 1/2 gallons
jello salad	3/4 gallon	1 1/4 gallons	2 1/2 gallons
potato salad	4 1/4 quarts	2 1/4 gallons	4 1/2 gallons
scalloped potatoes	4 1/2 quarts or 1 12" x 20" pan	9 quarts or 2 1/4 gallons	18 quarts 4 1/2 gallons
spaghetti	1 1/4 gallons	2 1/2 gallons	5 gallons
Sandwiches:			
bread	50 slices or 3 1-pound loaves	100 slices or 6 1-pound loaves	200 slices or 12 1-pound loaves
butter	1/2 pound	1 pound	2 pounds
lettuce	1 1/2 heads	3 heads	6 heads
mayonnaise	1 cup	2 cups	4 cups
mixed filling			
meat, eggs, fish	1 1/2 quarts	3 quarts	6 quarts
jam, jelly	1 quart	2 quarts	4 quarts

Microwave Hints

1. Place an open box of hardened brown sugar in the microwave oven with 1 cup hot water. Microwave on high for 1 1/2 to 2 minutes for 1/2 pound or 2 to 3 minutes for 1 pound.

2. Soften hard ice cream by microwaving at 30% power. One pint will take 15 to 30 seconds; one quart, 30-45 seconds; and one-half gallon, 45-60 seconds.

3. To melt chocolate, place 1/2 pound in glass bowl or measuring cup. Melt uncovered at 50% power for 3-4 minutes; stir after 2 minutes.

4. Soften one 8-ounce package of cream cheese by microwaving at 30% power for 2 to 2 1/2 minutes. One 3-ounce package of cream cheese will soften in 1 1/2 to 2 minutes.

5. A 4 1/2 ounce carton of whipped topping will thaw in 1 minute on the defrost setting. Whipped topping should be slightly firm in the center, but it will blend well when stirred. Do not over thaw!

6. Soften jello that has set up too hard - perhaps you were to chill it until slightly thickened and forgot it. Heat on a low power setting for a very short time.

7. Heat hot packs. A wet fingertip towel will take about 25 seconds. It depends on the temperature of the water used to wet the towel.

8. To scald milk, cook 1 cup for 2 to 2 1/2 minutes, stirring once each minute.

9. To make dry bread crumbs, cut 6 slices of bread into 1/2-inch cubes. Microwave in 3-quart casserole 6-7 minutes, or until dry, stirring after 3 minutes. Crush in blender.

10. Refresh stale potato chips, crackers or other snacks of such type by putting a plateful in the microwave for 30-45 seconds. Let stand for 1 minute to crisp. Cereals can also be crisped.

11. Nuts will be easier to shell if you place 2 cups of nuts in a 1-quart casserole with 1 cup of water. Cook for 4 to 5 minutes and the nutmeats will slip out whole after cracking the shell.

12. Stamp collectors can place a few drops of water on a stamp to remove it from an envelope. Heat in the microwave for 20 seconds, and the stamp will come off.

13. Using a round dish instead of a square one eliminates overcooked corners in baking cakes.

14. Sprinkle a layer of medium, finely chopped walnuts evenly onto the bottom and side of a ring pan or bundt cake pan to enhances the looks and eating quality. Pour in batter and microwave as recipe directs.

15. Do not salt foods on the surface as it causes dehydration and toughens food. Salt after you remove from the oven unless the recipe calls for using salt in the mixture.

16. Heat left-over custard and use it as frosting for a cake.

17. Melt marshmallow cream. Half of a 7-ounce jar will melt in 35-40 seconds on high. Stir to blend.

18. To toast coconut, spread 1/2 cup coconut in a pie plate and cook for 3-4 minutes, stirring every 30 seconds after 2 minutes. Watch closely, as it quickly browns.

19. To melt crystallized honey, heat uncovered jar on high for 30-45 seconds. If jar is large, repeat.

20. One stick of butter or margarine will soften in 1 minute when microwaved at 20% power.

Calorie Counter

Beverages

apple juice, 6 oz. 90
coffee (black) 0
cola type, 12 oz. 115
cranberry juice, 6 oz. 115
ginger ale, 12 oz. 115
grape juice, (prepared from
frozen concentrate), 6 oz. 142
lemonade, (prepared from
frozen concentrate), 6 oz. 85
milk, protein fortified, 1 c. 105
skim, 1 c. 90
whole, 1 c. 160
orange juice, 6 oz. 85
pineapple juice, unsweetened, 6 oz.......95
root beer, 12 oz. 150
tonic (quinine water) 12 oz. 132

Breads

cornbread, 1 sm. square 130
dumplings, 1 med. 70
French toast, 1 slice 135
melba toast, 1 slice 25
muffins, blueberry, 1 muffin 110
bran, 1 muffin 106
corn, 1 muffin 125
English, 1 muffin 280
pancakes, 1 (4-in.) 60
pumpernickel, 1 slice 75
rye, 1 slice 60
waffle, 1 216
white, 1 slice 60-70
whole wheat, 1 slice 55-65

Cereals

cornflakes, 1 c. 105
cream of wheat, 1 c. 120
oatmeal, 1 c. 148
rice flakes, 1 c. 105
shredded wheat, 1 biscuit 100
sugar krisps, 3/4 c. 110

Crackers

graham, 1 cracker 15-30
rye crisp, 1 cracker 35
saltine, 1 cracker 17-20
wheat thins, 1 cracker 9

Dairy Products

butter or margarine, 1 T. 100
cheese, American, 1 oz. 100
camembert, 1 oz. 85
cheddar, 1 oz. 115
cottage cheese, 1 oz. 30
mozzarella, 1 oz. 90
parmesan, 1 oz. 130
ricotta, 1 oz. 50
roquefort, 1 oz. 105
Swiss, 1 oz. 105
cream, light, 1 T. 30
heavy, 1 T. 55
sour, 1 T. 45
hot chocolate, with milk, 1 c. 277
milk chocolate, 1 oz. 145-155
yogurt
made w/ whole milk, 1 c. 150-165
made w/ skimmed milk, 1 c. 125

Eggs

fried, 1 lg. 100
poached or boiled, 1 lg. 75-80
scrambled or in omelet, 1 lg. 110-130

Fish and Seafood

bass, 4 oz. 105
salmon, broiled or baked, 3 oz. 155
sardines, canned in oil, 3 oz. 170
trout, fried, 3 1/2 oz. 220
tuna, in oil, 3 oz. 170
in water, 3 oz. 110

Calorie Counter

Fruits

apple, 1 med. 80-100
applesauce, sweetened, 1/2 c. 90-115
  unsweetened, 1/2 c...........................50
banana, 1 med. 85
blueberries, 1/2 c.....................................45
cantaloupe, 1/2 c......................................24
cherries (pitted), raw, 1/2 c. 40
grapefruit, 1/2 med. 55
grapes, 1/2 c. 35-55
honeydew, 1/2 c. 55
mango, 1 med. 90
orange, 1 med. 65-75
peach, 1 med. 35
pear, 1 med. 60-100
pineapple, fresh, 1/2 c............................40
  canned in syrup, 1/2 c. 95
plum, 1 med. 30
strawberries, fresh, 1/2 c.......................30
  frozen and sweetened, 1/2 c. 120-140
tangerine, 1 lg. 39
watermelon, 1/2 c. 42

Meat and Poultry

beef, ground (lean), 3 oz. 185
  roast, 3 oz. 185
chicken, broiled, 3 oz. 115
lamb chop (lean), 3 oz. 175-200
steak, sirloin, 3 oz. 175
  tenderloin, 3 oz. 174
  top round, 3 oz. 162
turkey, dark meat, 3 oz. 175
  white meat, 3 oz. 150
veal, cutlet, 3 oz...................................156
  roast, 3 oz. 76

Nuts

almonds, 2 T. 105
cashews, 2 T. 100
peanuts, 2 T. 105
peanut butter, 1 T. 95
pecans, 2 T. 95
pistachios, 2 T. 92
walnuts, 2 T. 80

Pasta

macaroni or spaghetti,
  cooked, 3/4 c. 115

Salad Dressings

blue cheese, 1 T. 70
French, 1 T. 65
Italian, 1 T. 80
mayonnaise, 1 T. 100
olive oil, 1 T. 124
Russian, 1 T. 70
salad oil, 1 T. 120

Soups

bean, 1 c. 130-180
beef noodle, 1 c. 70
bouillon and consomme, 1 c. 30
chicken noodle, 1 c. 65
chicken with rice, 1 c. 50
minestrone, 1 c. 80-150
split pea, 1 c. 145-170
tomato with milk, 1 c. 170
vegetable, 1 c. 80-100

Vegetables

asparagus, 1 c. 35
broccoli, cooked, 1/2 c. 25
cabbage, cooked, 1/2 c. 15-20
carrots, cooked, 1/2 c.......................25-30
cauliflower, 1/2 c. 10-15
corn (kernels), 1/2 c. 70
green beans, 1 c. 30
lettuce, shredded, 1/2 c..............................5
mushrooms, canned, 1/2 c. 20
onions, cooked, 1/2 c. 30
peas, cooked, 1/2 c...................................60
potato, baked, 1 med. 90
  chips, 8-10 100
  mashed, w/milk & butter, 1 c. ..200-300
spinach, 1 c. 40
tomato, raw, 1 med. 25
  cooked, 1/2 c. 30

Cooking Terms

Au gratin: Topped with crumbs and/or cheese and browned in oven or under broiler.

Au jus: Served in its own juices.

Baste: To moisten foods during cooking with pan drippings or special sauce in order to add flavor and prevent drying.

Bisque: A thick cream soup.

Blanch: To immerse in rapidly boiling water and allow to cook slightly.

Cream: To soften a fat, especially butter, by beating it at room temperature. Butter and sugar are often creamed together, making a smooth, soft paste.

Crimp: To seal the edges of a two-crust pie either by pinching them at intervals with the fingers or by pressing them together with the tines of a fork.

Crudites: An assortment of raw vegetables (i.e. carrots, broccoli, celery, mushrooms) that is served as an hors d'oeuvre, often accompanied by a dip.

Degrease: To remove fat from the surface of stews, soups, or stock. Usually cooled in the refrigerator so that fat hardens and is easily removed.

Dredge: To coat lightly with flour, cornmeal, etc.

Entree: The main course.

Fold: To incorporate a delicate substance, such as whipped cream or beaten egg whites, into another substance without releasing air bubbles. A spatula is used to gently bring part of the mixture from the bottom of the bowl to the top. The process is repeated, while slowly rotating the bowl, until the ingredients are thoroughly blended.

Glaze: To cover with a glossy coating, such as a melted and somewhat diluted jelly for fruit desserts.

Julienne: To cut vegetables, fruits, or cheeses into match-shaped slivers.

Marinate: To allow food to stand in a liquid in order to tenderize or to add flavor.

Meuniére: Dredged with flour and sautéed in butter.

Mince: To chop food into very small pieces.

Parboil: To boil until partially cooked; to blanch. Usually final cooking in a seasoned sauce follows this procedure.

Pare: To remove the outermost skin of a fruit or vegetable.

Poach: To cook gently in hot liquid kept just below the boiling point.

Purée: To mash foods by hand by rubbing through a sieve or food mill, or by whirling in a blender or food processor until perfectly smooth.

Refresh: To run cold water over food that has been parboiled in order to stop the cooking process quickly.

Sauté: To cook and/or brown food in a small quantity of hot shortening.

Scald: To heat to just below the boiling point, when tiny bubbles appear at the edge of the saucepan.

Simmer: To cook in liquid just below the boiling point. The surface of the liquid should be barely moving, broken from time to time by slowly rising bubbles.

Steep: To let food stand in hot liquid in order to extract or to enhance flavor, like tea in hot water or poached fruit in sugar syrup.

Toss: To combine ingredients with a repeated lifting motion.

Whip: To beat rapidly in order to incorporate air and produce expansion, as in heavy cream or egg whites.